All works are printed with permission from their original authors

All works copyright their original authors

Cover by Erin Gleeson

Edited by Paul Tyng

Thinking Beard Press – Baltimore - 2010

The Un Saddest Factory Presents a 10 Minute Play Festival

August 2010 – Volume 1

Table of Contents

Trio Bravo _____ 5

It Ain't Me Babe _____ 19

All You Have To Do Is-- _____ 30

Enter, Exit, Kiss, Fight, Die _____ 44

Original Papers by the Guilford Garden Club _____ 57

Crusaders _____ 71

Birdshit _____ 82

Getting Nailed Down _____ 95

An Annotated Guide to a Normal Conversation, or: This Cake Is Delicious! _____ 112

The Mysterious Occurrence in the House of Camille; 2010 World Almanac _____ 131

Trio Bravo

A Western in One Act

by R. M. O'Brien

CHARACTERS

Ned Pickett: Outlaw, leader of the Deletionists.

Crab Miller: Sheriff of Golgotha.

Sue Ann Sullivan: Sharpshooter.

Jim Cloud: Drunk. half-Indian.

Gray Eagle: Omnipresent Indian chief.

Also Narrator, Bartender, Barfly, & three Deletionists.

SETTING
Golgotha, West Texas.

TIME
Late 1800s.

Scene 1   Saloon. Good Friday.

Scene 2   Desert. Jail. Holy Saturday.

Scene 3   Jail. Easter Sunday.

PROLOGUE

NARRATOR

Ned Pickett was a bad man in a country full of bad men. There was something rotted inside of 'im—something worse'n in normal men—and he didn't try to hide it or humilify himself for it like a Christian. No, Ned wore his rot-awful soul on the outside, with PRIDE, like the devil himself.

He wasn't awful smart—he didn't much have to be. When a man is willing to cross just about every line of human decency—it gives him an advantage over average men bound by their consciences so he barely needs smarts at all. It can even make him seem uncanny, invincible to the meek. It was this way with Ned.

He had a three-man gang he called Deletionists. (& thank Christ he was uglier 'n shit or it'd a been bigger.) They raised hell all over West Texas, but mostly slept, drank, & fucked in the small tourist town of Golgotha, where the locals are all merchants of some kind or another, which is to say, more interested in their own self-preservation than in something as potentially unprofitable as justice or heroics. This worked well for the Deletionists for a time.

Now, hellbent on complicating things for Ned & his amigos was one Crab Miller, Golgotha's sheriff. Crab was as upright & altruistic as his fellow Golgothans were timid and mercenary. He was maybe the only man in the whole town who valued anything more than his own comfort. & he was downright religious in his pursuit to bring down Ned Pickett & the Deletionists. For Crab, defeating Ned was as good as destroying all the bad stuff inside his own self just like it never existed in the first place. Further, it would prove somethin' that Crab was keen on provin': that he was a good man.

Now, without makin' this whole story too complicated before it begins, Ned & his gang had been missing from Golgotha for nigh on a year, and while he was gone there came a price on his head, wanted alive. It was just Crab's luck that a vengeful girlfriend of Ned's was hot to see him arrested. That's how he came upon the special knowledge that Ned would be back in town for one night only, & that's the night our story starts.

SCENE ONE — "GOOD FRIDAY"

(A crowded, noisy saloon. JIM, SUE ANN, townsfolk.)

(NED is dragged onto the stage by DELETIONISTS 1, 2, & 3, and falls dead on his back. A tomahawk in his neck & bloody.)

DEL. 1

Get a doctor!

BARTENDER

A doctor? Get a coroner.

DEL. 2

Get the sheriff. Tell 'im Ned Pickett's dead!

(DEL. 3 hesitates.)

Do it!

(Exit DEL. 3.)

BARTENDER

Who did this?

DEL. 1

It was that damned injun Gray Eagle!

(Enter CRAB & DEL 3.)

DEL. 2

Sheriff, Ned got killed.

DEL. 3

It was Gray Eagle who done it.

CRAB

Are you sure it was Gray Eagle?

DEL. 1

It's a goddamned tomahawk at his throat!

DEL. 3

Yeah. Is you blind?

BARFLY

You've got to stop him, Sheriff. You've got to go out after him. Is this a town where the Indians get to pick off anyone they want?!

CRAB

Now hold up!

BARTENDER

Who'll stop off here on their way to Albuquerque if it's open season on white folks? You gotta consider the economics of the justice of the thing!

CRAB

(he has had it!)

Now I can't just go tearing all over West Texas starting an Indian war 'cause some murderin' scum wound up with a hatchet in his neck!

(Enter GRAY EAGLE offstage. His presence signalled by a lighting or sound cue.)

GRAY EAGLE

You will not have to go tearing all over nowhere to find me. I am here.

(EVERYONE looks to CRAB.)

CRAB

(stern)

Now Gray Eagle. You're going to have to come down to my office and give a statement.

GRAY EAGLE

I give you my statement now. I killed the white man. & I will kill the other three.

DEL. 2

Shit!

CRAB

Then, Gray Eagle, I am placing you under arrest for the murder of Ned Pickett.

GRAY EAGLE

That man & his gang killed one of our children

(Pause.)

I am only after the men who call themselves the Deletionists. This is no war with you, but woe to the man who stands in my way.

(Exit GRAY EAGLE.)

CRAB

(thinks for a second)

Okay. This is the way it is. I'll go after 'im like you want. But it'll take more 'n just me. Who's up for it?

>(Pause.)

>>SUE ANN

>>>(stepping forward)

Sue Ann Sullivan, sharpshooter. I hold more medals than any man or woman in five states.

>>CRAB

Well all right.

>>BARFLY

>>>(laughing)

You're a marksman?!

>>(All the assholes in the bar laugh.)

>>SUE ANN

Don't nobody move.

>>(SUE ANN fires off trick shot after trick shot in rapid succession. Glasses exploding, cigarettes shot out of hands, &c.)

>>CRAB

Okay shit Jesus. Who else?

>>JIM

>>>(slurring)

Jim Cloud, professional trapper.

>>(JIM falls through a table. Picks himself back up.)

BARTENDER

Professional drunk!

BARFLY

Yeah. Good luck, Sheriff.

BARTENDER

He's half Injun, half Irish, Crab. You're fucked!

CRAB

Yeah well he'll sober up tomorrow, when you all 'll still be just as yellow. Anyone else?

(Pause.)

All right.

(Pause.)

Deletionists. You're going to jail.

DEL. 3

The hell we are!

CRAB

Would you rather be left to him that ain't never heard of habeas corpus?! You'll be safer in a goddam jail cell anyway . . . safer 'n you'd be on the outside!

(DELETIONISTS look at each other, conferring.)

DEL. 3

We'll go like you said.

SCENE TWO — "HOLY SATURDAY"

(Blackout.)

> (An overhead projection reads, "HOLY SATURDAY".)

NARRATOR

And so Crab had assembled his Trio Bravo.

In the morning, he went out into the desert to find Gray Eagle's camp, bringing Jim along with 'im. Figured a half-Indian'd be of some help in finding the camp and reasoning with Gray Eagle. Sue Ann stayed back at the jail guarding the rest of the Deletionists. That Indian was wily; they couldn't afford to take any chances.

When Crab & Jim made it to the camp, Gray Eagle was away, but after some ordeal findin' one who spoke English, they left a message for him, amounted to he had a day to turn himself in and let a jury decide if what he done was warranted, that this was America, and there was a way you did things here, and there was a way you didn't ever do things. And they left and headed back through the desert toward town . . .

> (Lights up.)
>
> (The desert.)
>
> (Enter CRAB & JIM.)
>
> (CRAB, tired, takes a seat on a rock. JIM looks off into the distance, orienting himself.)

CRAB

Some kind of weird beauty to it, sure, but how could you stand living in a place that's the damn same everywhere you look?

> (Pause.)

How you doin', Jim?

JIM

Thirsty . . .

(pointing)

I think this is the way back.

CRAB

Well shit, Jim. Shouldn't you just know?

JIM

I'm not magic . . . I'm more white than Indian, anyway.

CRAB

Hey now, what's all that way off in the distance?

JIM

What? Nothing. More of the same.

CRAB

I'm bein' swept up in it.

JIM

Sheriff, your brain's just overheating.

CRAB

I'm back in my mother's womb, I'm leavin' it, but I'm not bein' birthed, I'm bein' shat out instead, I'm bein' born all wrong. I'm a monster, the cactuses are arrayed against me, I'm the only man in the universe. My guns, Jim! My guns are hawks & I am hateful to them, where are my guns? I could grab for 'em but they just beat their wings against me & blow me away. I gotta let 'em go! Shit! I don't have any teeth. Whyncha tell me I dint have any teeth? . . . The hawks are spittin' em up one by one, they're spittin' up my damn teeth . . . this is a wretched place, Jim.

JIM

Yeah let's leave it. We're not here on a vision-quest.

CRAB

The injuns have cursed the soil beneath our feet. It's everywhere I look. It's too late, now.

JIM

Well stop lookin' . . . & have a pull off my canteen. We gotta get to town, either way, so just close your eyes and let's keep moving.

(Exit JIM & CRAB.)

(Back at the jail. SUE ANN is tied up. The three Deletionists are dead.)

(Enter CRAB & JIM.)

CRAB

Sue Ann! What in the hell happened!

(JIM & CRAB begin to untie SUE ANN.)

SUE ANN

(somewhat frantic)

Gray Eagle . . . he came here with his Indians. I rose to meet 'em. They threw a deck of playing cards in the air to create confusion. I put five bullets through the Ace of Spades and levelled my Winchester at Gray Eagle's chest. There were too many of them. They pulled the keys off my neck and dragged the Deletionists out of their cell & executed 'em right in front of me!

(CRAB shoots once at the ceiling.)

CRAB

Goddammit!

SUE ANN

I shot every feather out of his hair, but my bullets missed his heart! It was like he was a ghost, or I was.

JIM

Well they're sure dead. I guess this fight is over.

CRAB

Nothin's over. We'll hole up here tonight. We'll bring the war to Gray Eagle tomorrow. We'll get him. We'll get every last one of 'em.

SCENE THREE — "EASTER SUNDAY"

> (Blackout.)
>
> (Overhead projection reads "EASTER SUNDAY".)

NARRATOR

So hole up they did, but contrary to their plans, Gray Eagle brought the war to them at dawn, announcing his presence & the presence of his men, from out of sight. And the Trio Bravo found themselves sunblind and surrounded.

> (Lights up.)
>
> (The jail. CRAB, JIM, & SUE ANN stand with their backs to the audience. CRAB peering out the bars of the door, JIM & SUE ANN flanking him, each looking out a barred window, guns ready. CRAB occasionally faces the audience; JIM & SUE ANN do not.)

SUE ANN

Some movement on top of that building over to my left.

                    (shoots)

Damn.

                    CRAB

Now just come on now & turn yourself in. You can't kill four men and expect to escape justice.

                    GRAY EAGLE

I was the agent of justice.

                    CRAB

We got plenty o' rounds o' ammunition in here! Enough to put twenty bullets in every man you've got!

                    GRAY EAGLE

You are a true white man. For safety you have put yourself in jail. Only the white man could feel safe in a prison. Because all his buildings are prisons or fortresses, because he is building them on land that does not belong to him, on land that is hostile to him. The stones & earth cry out against you. You cannot hear them.

                    CRAB

If you don't turn yourself in, you put your whole people at risk.

                    GRAY EAGLE

I do not heed the words of a dead man.

                    CRAB

Not dead yet, Goddammit!

                    GRAY EAGLE

Yes. You are already dead. All of you. Your Indian is under the spell of fire-water. He trades his heritage for bad dreams & dull reflexes; and the woman learns the skills of death for decoration. Her bullets find every feather in my hair . . . but her bullets miss my heart—

CRAB

Don't listen to 'im, just keep a close watch!

JIM

I can't see a damn thing!

GRAY EAGLE

. . . These arrows will not miss them. We do not even need to aim. For the seeds of these arrows have been growing inside them since their unclean births—

JIM

Where the hell are they?! Why can't I see 'em?!

SUE ANN

Steady yr hand, steady yr eye.

GRAY EAGLE

. . . When it is time, the arrows will bloom from their chests like desert roses.

(The sound of many arrows in flight.)

(SUE ANN & JIM fall away dead from their respective windows, an incredible number of arrows in each of their chests.)

(CRAB turns around.)

CRAB

Lord Jesus . . .

GRAY EAGLE

And Death will likewise bloom in your chest.

CRAB

May-be. But it 'll be by my watch and no other man's.

(Exit CRAB.)

NARRATOR

Sometimes a man finds himself truly desperate, & the only thing he can do and stay a man is run headlong into the unknown. And that's what Crab did: curst, half-mad Crab Miller ran straight outta that jail with nothing but his six-shooter and a prick, hard for death . . . And he got what he was looking for, one way or another.

It Ain't Me Babe

by Carrie Keith

Characters

Freida: Wears a homemade angel costume with detachable wings. Her movements are uncoordinated but graceful. Her delivery is free and easy.

Shakey: Dresses like young Rocky Erickson. He is disheveled, oblivious, sensitive and mostly out of his mind.

Notes

The changes in tone are rapid, frequent and sincere.

The transition between scenes should happen as quickly as possible.

SCENE ONE

(Dim lights. Freida's bed is center stage, nothing fancy- blankets on the floor and a bedside lamp. Freida undresses and crawls into bed.)

FREIDA

I know what's coming. It's living all over me. I'm thinking about it even when I'm not thinking. It's like a rat that crawls through the walls and dies. Ya can't see him but you can sense him. The thought crawled into my head and died there. The smell of death makes my eyes sting. I was weepy but I'm not now. Like I say, I know what's coming. I have traced the pattern in my mind. I started at the beginning and I know where it ends.

(Slight pause.)

What a terrible thought.

(Pause.)

What a strange world.

SHAKEY

(From off stage and in a soft voice.)

Why? What is so strange?

FREIDA

The feeling I've out lived the thing and at the same time knowing it's still to come. The feeling and knowing don't agree, like walkin' on water. Feels more like a dream. But it's not. Not a dream.

(Black out.)

(Silence.)

(Phone rings.)

FREIDA

Hello?

(Pause.)

I am awake.

(Silence.)

I don't want to talk about it.

(Silence.)

I'm here. I'm listening.

(Listening.)

Well I see it differently- You are not only weak or always strong. Make the decision then make it right. That's not scary. Scary's when you give up.

(Silence.)

Happiness is work. SHIT, SHAKEY, what the hell do you think? I've already made my decision. I'M IN IT. You decide.

(Pause.)

Sigh.

You hate everything.

(Crashing noise.)

Dammit!

I'm bleeding.

No.

I'm okay.

I'll be right over.

> (Freida turns on the bedside lamp, the only light source at this point. She climbs out of bed and dresses in a hurry. She looks around to see if she has forgotten anything, goes to leave, comes back and turns off the light.)

(Black.)

(Move bed and lamp off stage.)

SCENE TWO

> (House lights up.
> Freida paces through

> the audience, or somewhere that is not the stage.)

FREIDA

> (To herself but not mumbling.)

This place is as good as any. I went through all my disasters here. I know my neighbors and the checkers at the grocery store. Why should I trade them in for new ones, go somewhere else with you, when you hate it everywhere? The geographical cure...

Move the pain out of sight.

The inertia kills me. How many ways can you toast a piece of fucking bread?

What's happened to us?

> (Sarcastically.)

I can do better.

> (Mocking.)

I can do better.

> (In earnest.)

I can do better.

> (Freida exits.)
>
> (Black out.)

SCENE THREE

> (Very bright lights come up. Shakey is slumped into a chair, curled over himself, head down, his

>fingers pulling his eye lids closed and his fists rubbing his eye sockets. Words and sounds come out of him out of key and out of rhythm.)

SHAKEY

Fuck.

That.

No. Don't...

Stay.

> (He shivers and shakes and tears up.)
>
> (Lights move around, go off and on.)
>
> (Total panic.)

I just want to see the light.

> (He demonstrates what that would look like by holding his hands to his temples and gesticulating like an officer.)
>
> (The lights shine steady into Shakey's eyes.)
>
> (He sings)

"Sometimes the lights all shinning on me/ other times I can barely see."

Fuck! Why won't you just make out with me?

> (Freida enters. She is preoccupied with the wing that's tangled in her hair.)

She floats around the room, unaffected by Shakey.

SHAKEY

Make out with me, get it over with! Then we can all go home.

> (Watching Frieda while she works on untangling herself.)

Sometimes I want to strangle you!

> (Relaxing a little.)

Do you want me to do that for you?

FREIDA

No, I can manage, this happens all the time.

> (Setting her wings free she moves around the stage like a dancer warming up, but briefly.)

> (Shakey glares and follows her movement. As she goes on he becomes more obscene and desperate.)

> (Freida centers herself downstage center.)

FREIDA

> (Addressing the audience.)

Would it embarrass you very much if I told you that I love you?

> (She clears her throat, looks into the light.)

It is with the greatest honor that I bare the saddest news...

> (She shuts her eyes and hangs her head for a split second then recomposes herself.)

Our beautiful, courageous Maid of Orleans--

SHAKEY

GAWD!

Aren't you going to say anything?

I've laid it all out for you, EVERYTHING!

And I get NOTHING? I can't take it.

> (Shakey stands erect but looks like he is going to keel over. Eyes big and wild. He's puffed up like he's been stung.)

I have to go. I'm panicking. I'm going.

> (He makes motions of leaving but doesn't.)

I have no one- nothing to go to.

FREIDA

I am here. But if you'd rather be alone-

SHAKEY

ALONE, I am alone!

> (Lights down.)

> (Freida exits.)

SCENE FOUR

> (Lights up. Shakey stands alone.)

SHAKEY

I know it never works out, but in the end. People leave and that's always bad timing.

FREIDA

> (From off stage.)

You don't make it easy.

SHAKEY

What kind of way is that to start a conversation?

I'm not trying to make it easy. I'm not trying to make it hard.

> (Freida enters.)

FREIDA

> (Alternating between uncannily cool and full on rage.)

Shakey, you have The Goddamned Fourth of July parading through your skull. There's so much Racket it's drownin' me, makin' it hard to breath. You got some big ideas about how you want me that got nothing to do with me and everything to do with you.

SHAKEY

> (Laughs. Laughs hysterically. Drops to his knees and ends in the fetus position.)

I'm fucked.

I live the wrong way Freida.

I threw it all away.

You don't understand...

I'm so fucked.

> (Freida kneels at his side speaking in a low voice, comforting him.)
>
> (Lights fade to black.)
>
> (Shakey exits.)

SCENE FIVE

>(Lights up. Freida is in exactly the same position as before, motionless.)

(Silence.)

(Freida rises to her feet and paces the stage.)

FREIDA

I shut the blinds 'cus I wanted the light to quit. Just outside my window stood our past, staring me straight in the eye. Some folks look out to birds and gardens. Every time I looked out I was looking back. The mind can play some dirty tricks. I have to stay quick on my toes.

When my love goes I use a bottle of bleach and a fine point to remove each step.

I can show you just what I mean. I have it all prepared. It was going to be a surprise but the day is ruined, there will be no surprises.

Shakey, where'd you go?

Can you bring out the viewing screen?

>(Silence.)

Please?

>(Shakey enters and sits down.)

SHAKEY

Uhhhhhh...........

FREIDA

Did you bring the screen?

SHAKEY

Iiiiiittt's iiinnnah the car...

FREIDA

I want to show them my movie, can you grab it?

   (Shakey is unresponsive.)

Never mind I'll get it, where'd ya park?

SHAKEY

Uhhh...

   (Mumbles.)

   (Motions in a vague direction.)

   (Fumbles around in his pockets for the car keys.)

Where are my keys.

FREIDA

They're not in your pocket?

   (Shakey turns his pockets inside out.)

Did you leave them in the car?

SHAKEY

No I did not leave them in the car. I just had them.

FREIDA

Shakey, this is my moment to stage something outside our private hell and you're blowing it. You're crucifying me.

SHAKEY

Hell.

FREIDA

(To the audience.)

The function of the movie is-was, was like that of the tragic drama: above and beyond judgment and punishment, catharsis.

SHAKEY

Well.

You learn something new everyday-

That's all I've learned today.

> (Freida does a post modern dance that involves her trying to set fire to her wings. During which Shakey makes an awkward and long exit staring at things aimlessly and with more intent than those insignificant details call for.)

The End.

All You Have To Do Is--

a ten-minute play

by Rachel Monroe

CHARACTERS

DAD   A true believer. In full safari gear.

RUBY   AKA mom. The secret villain.

DASH   Calliope's younger brother, but still old enough to know better.

CALLIOPE   Fifteen. Full of doubt.

Note: the whole family speaks only in song, except for Calliope, who refuses to as of yesterday.

SETTING

This year, the family vacation/missionary trip is in the Amazon. There is an ambient sense of tropical heat, gaudy flora, strange creatures moving in bushes, restless natives with blowdarts, the whisper song of the keel-billed toucan, exploitation of natural resources, despotic rulers, drug cartels, and hidden caves, but all that we really need to see are some leaves. These leaves should give the impression of being huge, glossy, and unlike anything we've got here in the northern hemisphere. They should perhaps imply that jewel-colored bugs with many legs are lurking beneath. Overall, a sense of unfamiliarity and un-belonging.

TIME

Spring break, 2002. The afternoon of a long, long day.

SCENE ONE

(The hottest part of the afternoon. Calliope stands in one corner of

> the stage, looking nervously over her shoulder as she speaks furtively into a tape recorder.)

CALLIOPE

April 18, 2002. Family vacation-slash-missionary trip, day three. Location:

> (She scans the area, looking for clues. There are none. Just more of those leaves.)

Undetermined Amazon basin. GPS coordinates unavailable. Situation increasingly dire. Ruby excessively cheerful, possibly malarial. Dash pretending everything is okay. Guide has abandoned us. Supplies running low.

> (Hissing into recorder, more & more agitated)

And Dad is totally losing it, and—

> (Suddenly, the lights go red. Calliope looks alarmed, and crouches or ducks behind a tree or otherwise conceals herself. Dad enters, staggering theatrically. A radio or walkie-talkie is visible clipped to his belt, along with other explorer gear. He continues to flail around as he sings the following number.)

DAD

It burns! Oh how it burns,

And you'd think I might've learned

To just lay low, wait my turn

But no! I'll never learn.

So, okay, I had some grand ambitions

For this Amazonian family bonding expedition,

We'd save the natives through joyous song, okay,

And have a little fun along the way!

And then we lost the guide, it's true,

And as for the natives, we've got no clue

Or hint of their location, but that was just

A small frustration...

Then I woke up to a situation frankly dire

(And I'm no exaggerator or amplify-er!)

Because, my god! my skin's a-fire!

And yes, it burns! Oh how it burns!

It's some act of native spite or retribution,

A first step toward their revolution,

A sacrificial resolution!

And what if I end up fried, or poached instead

Or SCRAMBLED even, spread for breakfast on a hunk of native bread?

Because it burns! Oh how it burns!

(Having heard enough, Calliope jumps out and grabs her father by the shoulders, trying to shake some sense back into him. At the same time, the red lights turn off & we see that Dad is pink all over – badly sunburned.)

CALLIOPE

Dad! Snap out of it! There are no cannibals! No one's boiling you! You are sunburned!

DAD

(confused)

Funny, honey, but I can't hear ya,

Funny, honey, but I just don't understand,

Your mouth's a-movin' and the sound comes out,

Maybe it's Amazonian words you spout?

Maybe you've gone restless, native, heathen

Their secret poison perhaps you've eaten?

'Cause--

CALLIOPE

Dad!!! I'm speaking English, okay? Listen, I just don't feel like singing. There isn't a tune or anything but you can understand me, it's still all English words. Look, I don't want to spread the gospel of song, I just want to go home, okay? So can you give me the radio and I'll call someone?

DAD

(trying hard)

There's somethin' there,

Some sense or truth or fact, I swear

A lilting, distant, melodyyyyyy...

CALLIOPE
(coaxingly)

The radio, give me the radio, Dad.

DAD
(experimentally)

Ra-di-ooooo?

(Just when it seems like Calliope might be getting through, Ruby bursts in from the right with Dash trotting along behind her. Ruby has twigs in her hair, is disheveled underneath her cheery veneer. Dash is nervous, keeps sending Calliope pleading looks.)

RUBY

You found her!

DAD

I think she's sick – she isn't right.

RUBY

She's acting out.

DASH
(nervously plucking leaves from a tree)

Can we not fight?

DAD

Calliope, sing something for them.

RUBY

Young lady, there is no excuse—

DASH

Cally, all you've got to do is-

CALLIOPE

Look, I quit, I don't want to sing, I don't want to spread the gospel of song to the natives, I just want to go to high school, okay? Don't pretend you can't understand what I'm saying, either, because --

RUBY

(cutting her off)

She's gone insane, she's nuts, she's mad,

She's round the bend (it's very sad!),

She's batty, bonkers, she's a loon,

(I do hope she'll recover soon),

She's dippy, loco, she's out to lunch,

(I must admit, I've had a hunch...)

She's warped, she's bonkers, I'd call her wacky,

She's daft, and daffy, she's fruit loops, crackers!

There's bats in that belfry! Her screws are loose!

Her deck's not got all fifty-two!

She's lost her marbles – hell, she's gone so far

She doesn't know what marbles ARE –

(Calliope runs off stage in tears.)

SCENE TWO

> (It's two days later, and the family is a mess. Everyone is dirty, clothing's torn, they've all got crazed looks in their eyes. Calliope is tied to a tree. The other family members refuse to acknowledge this. Occasionally she'll struggle, but we get the idea that she's mostly given up. While Ruby sings, Dash & Dad are trying somewhat pathetically to take care of some jungle survival business, like making a fire or something.)

> RUBY

>> (optimistically, in a way that doesn't match the circumstances at all)

The poor cannibals of Brazil

Need a song to lift their hearts.

We have come in peace, good will,

We fear not spears nor poison darts,

We fear not madness, rage, or wrongs

As we lift our lightened hearts in song.

And I get a lovely, bubbly feeling

When I think of all the souls we'll save

... As soon as we can only find them

in their huts, or shacks, or caves.

We fear not madness or duress,

Nor killer bees, nor painful death,

For armed with music, joy, and love---

> (As her song builds to a crescendo, Calliope starts squirming.)

CALLIOPE

Hey! HEY! I fear bees! I fear painful death! Untie me! Lemme go!

RUBY

Oh, hello there sweetheart.

CALLIOPE

Look, just untie me. Please? I think this tree's got termites.

RUBY

Hmmm, I really do wish I could understand

A word you're saying. If you'd only sing.

That bark looks like the itchiest thing...

> (Dash stands up, walks over to his sister. He sings begrudgingly, but pleadingly. Meanwhile,

Ruby pulls out a piece of paper and starts writing on it.)

DASH

Calliope. I don't know why

You act like it's us who're the bad guys.

Just…sing a little. I know you can.

Then you know they'll understand--

Grab the radio, sing for help,

Then we get helicoptered out of here,

Come on, I know you can.

In just 2 years you'll be 18, and free,

You'll never have to sing again,

If you'll just keep singing until then.

Come on, I know you can--

CALLIOPE

Traitor!!!

(dejected, getting a little loopy)

I mean, I understand where you're coming from, I just find that I express myself better when I talk, you know, like a regular person. And then I don't have to worry about keeping the tune straight, or coming up with tortured rhymes. You guys should try it! Just for a little bit, you can still sing sometimes, you know, at birthday parties and stuff, when it's appropriate--

RUBY

Oh my. Those sounds.

Here, dear. Read this. Aloud.

> (Ruby gives Calliope a piece of paper, which Calliope proceeds to read aloud.)

CALLIOPE

Do, re, me, fa --- HEY!

DAD

> (leaps up)

A plan! A plan! I've got a plan!

I'll save us all

Well, just because I'm dad!

I'm dad, by golly, and I've got a plan!

> (Dash dashes over & claps him on the arm and Dad yelps, as he is still quite sunburned. But he's undaunted.)

We use Cally here as bait

And in the meantime, lurk nearby and wait.

Once we hear their hungry shouts,

We run over! We pop out! We quickly wow 'em,

The usual song and dance, etcetera,

Win their trust, earn some fans

Aaand... That's it! Hoo boy! I've got a plan!

I'm dad, by golly, and I've got a plan!

CALLIOPE

> (looking around for support)

You're kidding right? This is the worst idea I've ever heard. I mean, I don't believe in cannibals. Dash?

DASH

(anxious)

Well, I don't know.

Well, I'm not sure.

Well, I have doubts.

What if they eat her?

Or what if she's hurt?

Or what about scorpions, lepers, or gout?

Or voodoo witch doctors, or lightning, or drought?

What if we forget her?

Or get lost on the way?

What if she can't find something to eat?

And what about blisters, and chafing, and scrapes?

And did you consider she might swoon in the heat?

And what about--

(A not-so-distant sound of drums and/or yelling silences everyone. It sounds like cannibals, for sure. And they're approaching.)

RUBY, DASH, DAD

The cannibals!

CALLIOPE

(trying to convince herself)

There's no such thing as cannibals. Only in cartoons. Only in cartoons.

DAD

> (shouting, blustering through his nerves)

Cannibals! Do not approach in fear,

Or hunger,

For we are here as your human brothers

And sisters, or maybe more like close family friends.

The family of humanity! It never ends, we are all one!

And we don't eat our family, that'd be no fun,

So set down your spears and spikes and gun

And join us in a simple song of welcome and amends?

> (Mom joins in, & Dash too eventually)

Cannibals! We are your human brothers!

Cannibals! A simple song of welcome!

The family... of... humanity!

> (as they sing, the family strides slowly, bravely off stage, leaving Calliope tied to the tree. She struggles wildly for a while, but can't get loose. Eventually, she stops fighting.)

CALLIOPE

HEY CANNIBALS! Come on! Tender flesh here, abandoned and alone! Come and get me. WHATEVER!

(Her shouting is met by resounding silence. Perhaps an echo of Amazonian crickets. She slumps down, defeated. But wait! A rustling in the bushes. Calliope doesn't hear it, but we do – and then another rustling, and she lifts her head and stares at the bush. The AMAZONS emerge. They are wearing cool outfits, feathers, warpaint. They are silent and move in a spooky way. They look less hungry than wary. They circle Calliope, sniffing.)

Um, hello.

(Amazons recoil at the sound of her voice, but we get the sense that some mutual interest is developing. In the distance, we hear the singing of the family approach – they must be coming back. Calliope looks around, panicked.)

Hey, look, we don't have much time, okay? Some – some BAD people are coming, bad people who tied me up, and they are very powerful, and also completely horrifying. With multiple guns. You know guns?

(Amazons regarding her quizzically. Do they understand? Unclear.).

But what if you untie me, and I join up with you, okay? I know all their tricks, I can be very valuable in terms of evasive maneuvers.

(One Amazon squeaks)

I mean, I would prefer not to eat them, especially the small one –

(Amazon makes a skeptical noise. Family singing coming even closer.)

Look you just have to untie me, okay? I'm with you now. Promise. I feel good about it. You guys GET me, you know?

(One Amazon unties her. Another smears paint on her cheeks, and a third sticks feathers in her hair. Maybe a quick initiatory rite. As the family enters, singing/frightened, the Amazons close ranks around Calliope and her family doesn't notice her at first.)

FAMILY

Cannibals, we come in peace.

Cannibals, we bring you songs.

Sing along with us, all you have to do is siiiing... along.

Cannibals, we offer joy.

Cannibals, we mean no wrong.

Sing along with us, all you have to do is siiiing... along.

(etc)

DASH

(noticing)

Calliope?!

(The family is stunned into silence. The Amazons stomp their feet, then break into an awesome dance. It is over-the-top and kind of show-tuney and totally embarrassing. They chant or otherwise vocalize as they dance in unison. At first Calliope stands, stunned; then one of the Amazons elbows or pushes her, and she falls in step. The family staggers backward in awe, backing off stage, as Calliope becomes more and more into her Amazonian role....)

Enter, Exit, Kiss, Fight, Die

a ten-minute play

by Matthew Smith

Characters

A Special One   Several Ages

Woman   Mother, Stranger

Man   Father, First Love, Nurse

Setting

The world. This can be represented by a blank stage.

> (Darkness. ASO enters.
> A spotlight arrests her
> at center stage.
> Blinking, she takes a
> deep breath.)

ASO

Here I am! Sorry to keep you waiting... Ta-da! Well... You know me, I'm the one who's here. That's OK, you'll remember soon. It certainly is cold in here, and bright! What a shame. You know I prefer things warm and dark.

> (As WOMAN speaks, the spotlight fades and a
> softer yellow light rises on the stage at large.
> WOMAN stands, performing a simple task––
> fixing something, perhaps, or cleaning up.)

WOMAN

It's not too bright. Have a blanket. There.

ASO

Who's that?

WOMAN

I'm your mother.

ASO

Well, this is my mother, and as you already know, I'm the one who's here.

WOMAN

No, no, special one. It's not just you.

ASO

There are others. I see. So, here's my mother, I'm the special one...

WOMAN

Sweet, silly child, you bring me joy!

ASO

I know. Where was I? My mother's here...

WOMAN

What shall I call you?

ASO

...and here I am, the special one.

WOMAN

'A Special One.' I suppose that's what I'll call you. Now, run into the next room, A Special One. I've left a treat there just for you.

ASO

This treat I will accept, but what is a next room?

WOMAN

You'll find it, A Special One

ASO

Obviously, I'll find it, Mother.

> (ASO exits. WOMAN watches her go, then allows her smile to relax.)

WOMAN

'Mother'... Oh. When did I let all this happen? My Darling, when did I let this happen? Give me your hands against my back, the nape of my neck, My Darling. You know I prefer them holding me. I prefer them holding me to nothing, and now I have nothing. Is that you there in the back of the room? You look so different. You look like someone else. Me? I was prettier six years ago, thirty-six years ago. Without you around to look at me, I've forgotten what to look like. You know I hold it against you: your strong hands pressing my nape, your eyes, your greedy mouth, I hold it all against you. You were what I promised myself not to do without. I promised never to settle for less than you. And look what happened! A life of work and happiness and drooping skin. The hands of an old lady. Come back now. Bring me your hands against my back. You look just like a beautiful young stranger. Come back now. I must still be young!

> (ASO re-enters, confused, nearly distraught. She has apparently misplaced the blanket.)

ASO

You! You old thing, there you are! There was no treat, and you weren't there to protect me!

WOMAN

A Special One. Give me your face. Where's your blanket? You're all dirty.

ASO

Of course I'm dirty! Someone hit me. Someone hit me and said mean things to me and you weren't there to punish her.

WOMAN

Oh, Special One, I'm sorry.

ASO

Are you crying? What do you have to cry about?

WOMAN

Nothing, my Special One. Old things. Just things that happened before you were born.

ASO

Before I was born? That's what you thought about while I was getting hit? What's wrong with you?

WOMAN

I'm old. I'm old forever, and I'm going to leave. I'm sorry. I have to leave. I can't be here again.

ASO

That's nonsense. You're right here. Besides, I'm thinking of what I'd like for supper. I've never had supper before, you know. Now, make me something. You'll feel better. Maybe ketchup on a bun? Or sugar cereal?

WOMAN

I don't want to leave. I need this body. Now it hurts, but once it made men love me.

ASO

Men don't love bodies. Men love special ones. But also, what are men?

WOMAN

It doesn't matter right now, baby. Only that my body made them love me. I never noticed it before. A Special One, I have to leave.

ASO

Where's that?

WOMAN

Oh, no, no, no, no! I don't want to leave! How will I find My Darling?

(A man's voice echoes from offstage.)

MAN

Precious Girl! A Special One! Wait!

ASO

Who said that? Was that My Darling?

WOMAN

No, that was only A Favorite. He was your daddy. But he's going, too. We're almost gone.

ASO

What? Stop it! Why are you letting this happen?

WOMAN

I don't know.

(WOMAN exits. ASO stands alone onstage.)

ASO

Who will watch over me until she comes back?

> (MAN enters, confident, forceful. As he speaks, he removes his jacket and places it over ASO's shoulders.)

MAN

Look at you. Here, take this. You must be cold.

ASO

Your voice, it's just like my father's.

MAN

I'm sure he was a fine man.

ASO

Was? I didn't tell you he was dead.

MAN

Kiss me. You'll like it. Come on, give me a kiss.

> (He kisses her. She does not resist, though she is startled. This awkward contact resolves into an eager, willing clasp. They hold each other, kissing, for a long beat.)

ASO

What was that?

MAN

That's kissing. Give me another.

ASO

Yes, kissing I like. But what was it I said? Before. That word I called my father. Dead. What's that?

MAN

I don't know... Like, not here? In the next room?

ASO

That's not it. I've been to the next room. Dead is somewhere else. No place. Hm. I guess we'll never know. All right, give me some kisses now.

MAN

What do you mean, no place? No place at all? That's it? That's what I've been saying all this time? 'I'm sure he was a fine man?'

ASO

I guess so. Now more kisses.

MAN

Is that what happens? All the time, to strangers? Does that happen while we're in here kissing?

ASO

Maybe. I'm glad they're only strangers.

MAN

Then... someday there'll be others in here kissing while it's happening to us!

ASO

I wish you'd just stop saying things and kiss me like proper husband.

MAN

I'm not a husband.

ASO

But... you kissed me, and you're not my father. Who are you?

MAN

I'm just the first man you kiss in your life. I'm called Unique.

ASO

Unique? Who's going to be my husband?

MAN

Maybe the seventh man you kiss. Maybe no one. I don't know. I'm terrified.

ASO

Me, too.

MAN

Really? You have it, too? That sickening trapped feeling?

ASO

Don't leave me. Give me your hands against my back, the nape of my neck. Don't you know I prefer them holding me?

MAN

What are you talking about?

ASO

You're my own darling. I won't settle for less than you.

MAN

You'll feel different later. You're a woman. But the feelings I have won't change. They can't change.

ASO

I promise you I'll never change.

MAN

Listen. Before I go forever and don't see you ever again, there's something I want you to know.

(He exits.)

ASO

What? Why did he leave? What will I do now?

(A long pause. Nothing happens. The light changes gradually back to a spot.)

ASO

I felt sure something would happen just now.

(Another pause, not quite as long.)

ASO

There's been a miscalculation. I appear to be alone. It's an oversight. I'm sure you understand.

(WOMAN enters, dressed childishly.)

WOMAN

Oh. I was hoping for candy.

ASO

Who are you?

WOMAN

It can talk? Never mind, this is the best treat in the world!

ASO

Who are you?

WOMAN

What else can it say?

ASO

What else can what say?

WOMAN

Boring now. Well, come on. Mama is waiting.

ASO

Let go of me, you nasty little thing!

(WOMAN stops, stunned.)

WOMAN

I'm not a nasty thing. I'm One of a Kind. You're nasty. I hate this treat. Take it away!

ASO

Shut up! Who are are you talking to?

WOMAN

That's a mean word. Mama said––

(ASO strikes WOMAN, knocking her down. WOMAN stares up at ASO, more surprised than hurt.)

ASO

Don't you understand? You're not the only one here. Other people want things, too. They have their own treats to think about. Sometimes you just have to shut up and leave people alone. OK? And: I'm sorry. I did not at all mean to hit you that hard. You're OK, aren't you?

> (A pause. WOMAN sucks in a deep breath.)

WOMAN

I'm telling!

> (WOMAN runs off. ASO slouches, resigned. Nothing happens. MAN enters.)

MAN

There you are. You must be cold without a sweater.

ASO

There who is? Oh, you. Did you come back? You look so different. I can't tell if that's you or just a nice looking stranger.

MAN

Maybe it's me and I'm a nice looking stranger. Give me your arm.

ASO

My body's shy. I feel a little sick.

MAN

You are sick. You're very sick. Give me your arm.

ASO

Your hands feel strong, just like I promised myself. Would you like to be the second man I ever kiss?

MAN

That's kind, but I'm too young for you.

ASO

Too young? Too young for me? When did I have all of my babies?

MAN

A long time ago, I'm sure. How many do you have?

ASO

Not even one. I don't think even one. Is all that finished already?

MAN

I'm sure you would have made a wonderful mother.

ASO

You're so handsome and patient. You should have children. Find a girl like me. Pretty, and famous.

MAN

Thank you, I will try.

ASO

All right, tell my friends to come in now. Bring them in to see me. One of a Kind and Unique and Precious Girl. Or... no, that was my mother's name.

MAN

No one is out there. I'm very sorry.

ASO

Oh... It's just you, then. Will you stay with me?

MAN

It's my job to wait with you.

ASO

Thank you... Isn't it odd? Somebody must be kissing someone right this second.

MAN

That's a fine thought. Take good breaths now. It's almost time.

ASO

Almost time? How odd. Just think! Just think of all the things I must have done by now.

MAN

That's OK. Try to keep this wrapped around your shoulders. Easy, there's my hand. You're OK. It's almost time.

ASO

It's almost time. Just think of it! Why, I must be so happy.

(Curtain.)

Original Papers by the Guilford Garden Club

Unabridged version

by Liz Donadio & Steve Strohmeier

CHARACTERS

THE SPEAKER A man wearing an unassuming suit, perhaps a little threadbare. He is a ghost. Before his death the speaker was an avid member of several clubs and organizations. He keeps this hobby going from beyond the grave but takes it to a new level where he watches club participants intensely and knows all of the intimate and ordinary details about their lives.

MRS. RONALD T. ABERCROMBIE   Tall and lanky, her body is like a stem. Mrs. Abercrombie holds her head high and doesn't move much when she speaks. She stands very tall and straight and still. Others find her to be cold and elitist in her mannerisms but it's the only way she knows how to be. Whenever Mrs. Abercrombie tries to smile warmly, it looks like a painful grimace.

MRS. D. REESE MCNEILL   Mrs. McNeill looks a bit like a bird herself. But not a colorful, lively or cheery bird; she is more morose and gray-colored, like a mockingbird. Mrs. McNeill has a manic way of speaking and occasionally trails off as if something has upset her. She relates to the mockingbird's way of pretending to be something that it's not.

MRS. HELFENSTEIN Short in stature, Mrs. Helfenstein has wild hair and a warm disposition. She is a bit sloppy in the way she dresses but in a charming way. She can be scatter-brained and easily distracted. A lover of poetry, she holds a book with her that she reads her quotes from.

As she speaks about each garden odor she breathes in heavily as though the flower were right under her nose.

MRS. G. HARVEY BECK Mrs. Beck looks unassuming and plain, simply dressed in order to not stand out. Gardening has been her comfort, plants are her support and she cares for them like loved ones. It's not totally clear what she's been through that's made her rely on nature in this way but it was enough to cause her to close off from the rest of the world.

SETTING

An ordinary room. Four chairs are placed across the stage and a podium is at the center.

TIME

September 22, 1930.

ACT ONE

SCENE ONE

(MRS. ABERCROMBIE, MRS. HELFENSTEIN, MRS. MCNEILL, and MRS. BECK are seated, unmoving. SPEAKER enters and walks across the stage. He is holding a binder to his side which he places on the podium and addresses the audience. He has an almost bureaucratic air of easy formality — he is evidently doing something he has done many times before. He takes his time getting started. The Speaker's dialogue can be partially read from the binder due to its length, as well as the fact that his character is probably reading a prepared speech. However it should be directed outwards towards the audience. His general manner and speech, although reflecting the time in which the story takes place, are in stark contrast to the ladies, who should be portrayed in a very stylized manner, verging on caricature.)

SPEAKER

Greetings ladies and gentleman, and welcome to the bi-monthly meeting of the Guilford Garden Club. At this time I would ask you to please locate a seat if you haven't already, as we will soon be commencing with our program.

Before we begin I hope you will join me in showing our appreciation for today's date, September 22, the year of Our Lord nineteen hundred and thirty, as it marks the 23rd anniversary of the Garden Club, and as I look about the room I am overjoyed to see some faces that have been with us from the very start. It is these very souls who have planted the seeds and watered the soil of our collective interest all these years and it is to these that I humbly dedicate the honor of today's proceedings.

Without further ado I would like to present to you one of our most esteemed and founding caretakers, and the first speaker of this evening's program.

Mrs. Ronald T. Abercrombie, who will be discoursing on the topic of tulips tonight, is certainly no stranger to beauty. In fact, for the greater part of her life, she has been steadily formulating, through diverse and sundry experiences, an all-encompassing aesthetic of Beauty; one, which she feels, will ensure her a foothold in certain realms of immortality. The story of how Mrs. Abercrombie became so enamored with the idea of physical perfection is more common than one would think — a child of hard-working middle-class parents, she was taught to look down upon lower elements of society, and, at all costs, to strive to place herself above the disfiguring struggles of the peasant's life—a lesson she learned all too well when as a child of 4 years old she attempted to pick up a stray dog turd she had located under a park bench, and was caught by her mother and beaten heartily. "DIRTY!!" Her consumptive mother shouted as she slapped young Clara's wrist repeatedly, a word which would enter Mrs. Abercrombie's vocabulary for the rest of her life, to be deployed only when describing the most odious and detestable aspects of existence.

Young Clara found it difficult to marry, finding woefully inadequate the awkward, groping attempts of certain local suitors, who could never understand why she shrank away in such horror at her advances. She eventually settled for Mr. Ronald T. Abercrombie, a soap-salesman who would only purchase newspapers after selecting them from the middle of a stack, and who discussed endlessly his confusion at the human fascination with what he called "the sexual act." In nightmares, Mrs. Abercrombie, a stay-at-home wife with no children, imagines herself in dark stuffy rooms full of disembodied and unwashed hands.

Recently, a change has come over Mrs. Abercrombie, stemming from an incident that took place a silent movie theater on July 2, 1930. While sitting in the dark theater, hypnotized by the marvels of modern technology, she fell into a trance at the sight of Mary Pickford, silent movie star and "America's Sweetheart." As Ms. Pickford smiled coyly and mouthed words at the camera, Mrs. Abercrombie felt a sensation unknown to her, and indefinable in words. She only knew that in the light of Ms. Pickford's countenance, she felt as though she had finally found something wholly beautiful, wholly clean, something that combined all those rare and exotic elements not to be found in everyday life—moreover, something that transported her far above the huddled, sweating bodies herding themselves like cattle into the movie house that hot summer night.

The events that may have taken place, indeed the life that might have been led in the light of the revelations of that night constitute quite another story. But I have been woefully long-winded in my introduction — I ask you to excuse me if I break off here and present to you without further fanfare, Mrs. Ronald T. Abercrombie and her presentation, entitled simply (but beautifully!) "Tulips."

> (MRS. ABERCROMBIE stands and adjusts her hat. SPEAKER sits on the side of the stage to observe, looking down at his nails or adjusting his tie every once in awhile.)

MRS. ABERCROMBIE

The facts that I am going to give you on tulip history are correct, I think, as I have found the same in many books.

Tulips are originally from Persia and Asia Minor. They found their way to Europe through an ambassador of Emperor

Ferdinand I who saw them in Constantinople. They eventually came to Holland in the 17th century where the cultivation of tulips developed very quickly and became extremely popular.

Everybody who had a fair sized garden wanted tulips. Remarkable it is that at that time people valued most the variegated tulips, that is – red, pink, or purple flowers, white or yellow striped, or marbled. The more stripes the more valuable the tulip! It was a fine hobby, which, alas afterwards degenerated into gambling. All kinds of auctions were organized and the enormous amount of money paid for tulips made people invest their savings in bulbs. People of all trades: weavers, tailors, blacksmiths, etc., started bulb growing, trying to make a fortune quickly.

Such absurd trading led to the most serious excesses, and fortunately the States of Holland, in 1637, decided to stop this sort of thing and published their decision by giving out a proclamation. Hence, the cultivation of tulips could be developed along normal lines, which is what indeed happened. After many ups and downs, the present high standard was attained, and whosoever visits in spring the Dutch bulb nurseries must be struck by the wealth in form and color as well as by the long flowering season.

The two main types of tulips are the brilliant Cottage and older Breeder types. When bred together they create Darwins, which have a vigor of growth and substance of flower, and a brilliance in color which make them easily the finest of all late tulips.

Breeders are a trifle somber at times but always attractive. Bybloem tulips are striped and feathered rose or violet on white. Bizarre tulips are yellow with dark brown red feathering. The Parrot tulip takes it name from a supposed likeness of the flower in bud to the head of a parrot. The slashed edges of the petal are quite like parrot tail feathers, I think. They are shy bloomers, but very striking in color.

A well planted collection of tulips are little care and repay one a hundred fold, not alone in the joy they bring to us but also in the pleasure we pass on to others who are not so fortunate as to possess these lovely and abiding companions.

> (MRS. ABERCROMBIE exits the stage as SPEAKER rises and opens his binder to read about the next presenter.)

SPEAKER

Thank you Mrs. Abercrombie for that delightful first act in our humble proceedings. Let us hope that we can attain even a fraction of the grace and purity that suffuse the very essence of that mythic beauty, the tulip.

Our next speaker, Mrs. D. Reese McNeill, will be demonstrating her expertise in the field of ornithology, or the study of avian life, i.e. birds.

Mrs. McNeill has held a life-long interest in birds, and indeed in the broader category of animal-life in general. As a child, she was an avid collector of fauna —everything from insects to alley cats found temporary shelter in her room, and was subject to her probing yet maternal care. Her obsession with all things natural led her to certain less-than-social activities, such as the collecting and storing of mass quantities of her own hair and fingernails, as well as the harvesting of various forms of molding or rotten food, which would be studied triumphantly at regular intervals by the intrepid young scientist. Any unsuspecting human life-form that made its way into this cabinet of curiosities would be given an unsolicited and uncompromising tour of the many exhibits — most would not return for a second viewing.

Despite failing to connect emotionally with the squeamish human species, Mrs. McNeill eventually developed a gleeful attachment to her neighborhood mailman, Reese McNeill. Everyday upon delivering the mail Mr. McNeill would receive in exchange certain inedible baked goods, seemingly lacking in any sort of butter or sugar or egg and presented without fanfare in the outstretched cupped hand of the future Ms. McNeill. Though initially disturbed by this ritual, Mr. McNeill soon grew fond of his benefactor, and the two were married in the spring of 1912.

Though the life of a biologist was not one considered suitable for women in those days, Ms. McNeill maintained her interest in the animal kingdom by setting up one of Baltimore's first animal shelters, which she ran for a number of years before her complete refusal to euthanize even the most rabid and dangerous beasts set her at odds with her co-owners. In her later years though, her innate desire to care for the living reached a long and satisfying conclusion as her husband lapsed further and further into the outer reaches of Alzheimer's disease, during which time Mrs. McNeill took some joy in feeding him his dinner by spooning small bites into his upturned gullet, like a nesting swallow regurgitating the contents of its stomach into the eager beak of a waiting chick.

But I digress! How unfair of me to allow my simple introductions to ramble on so...ladies and gentlemen, please welcome Mrs. D. Reese McNeill, and her speech entitled "Some of My Experiences with Birds."

> (MRS. MCNEILL stands and approaches the podium tentatively. SPEAKER steps aside to let her pass and stands off to the side of the stage.)

> MRS. MCNEILL

Some years ago a beautiful mocking bird appeared in a wild cherry tree close to the house with an apparent longing for human companionship. The idea came to me that I might tame him a little, never dreaming that he would come into the house for food. Seedless raisins were placed on the windowsill and later on, on the sewing machine by the window. My husband and I would go from the room and watch him peering around the sewing machine trying to get enough courage to come in. He would sit around all day near us. Then we put raisins on the bathroom windowsill and sat quietly in the bedroom. When he grew bold enough to come inside and eat on the washstand we felt that much had been accomplished. Later on came the thrill of persuading him to come into my room and perch on the bedpost with the curious look of a young boy.

The bird was a joy for several years. He ate either in the living room or on my bed where a paper was spread for him. He loved to investigate. A vision of himself in a long mirror puzzled him. After flying at it several times he flew down to the floor and quietly walked around the door to look for the other bird. Not seeing one, he was then perfectly satisfied. Once when a window was left open he came in and flew across the hall to where several of us were talking in another room. He sat up on the mantelpiece and faint musical notes were heard, watching him we could see his little throat move.

After his life was over, we fed other birds as we did him but none were as trusting. There were two mockingbirds but they left us this summer and have not returned. I think that something happened to the pair.

> (MRS. MCNEILL exits with what looks like a
> heavy heart. SPEAKER quietly applauds.)

SPEAKER

I think we have all been instructed and fortified by Mrs. McNeill's profound understanding of those denizens of the earth's ether, the birds. Thank you, Mrs. McNeill, on behalf of all of us.

Ladies and gentleman, you may perhaps be wondering at this stage of tonight's proceedings, how exactly I came to possess such intimate information regarding our beloved speakers — especially that information that can only be described as temporally implausible. Although I'm afraid that I cannot satisfy your curiosity to the fullness of its desire, I will mention here that along with being a proud member of the Guilford Garden Club, I am also a member of several other Groups, some of a very curious nature, about which I am forbidden to speak lest I do harm to some of those most cherished beliefs of the human race vis-à-vis certain cosmic principles, theologies and the like et cetera et cetera...but what a bore I must be! I must apologize once again for these self-indulgent non-sequiturs. Now let me see...

> (SPEAKER rifles through his papers while MRS. HELFENSTEIN sneaks up behind him. She taps SPEAKER on the shoulder, which startles him as he turns around quickly.)

MRS. HELFENSTEIN

(With a hopeful tone in her voice.)

Is it my turn yet?

SPEAKER

(Warmly, with a hint of smugness.)

No, no, not quite my dear. Have patience and you'll get your chance soon enough.

> (MRS. HELFENSTEIN smiles thankfully, nods, and hurries back to her seat. SPEAKER turns back to the audience.)

Now that you've met our next speaker, Mrs. Helfenstein, I can tell you that she wishes with an all-consuming passion that she had been born in another era of human existence. Her mind is replete with the myths and legends of fallen empires, ancient civilizations and most of all — the biblical heroes of her beloved New Testament. There is a birthmark on the inside of her left thigh, a barely discernable cleft in her palette. She became fascinated with fragrance after a traumatic visit to the city of Chicago in 1885, at which time she became acquainted with the smell of boiled blood and excrement as it wafted across the city from the massive neighboring stockyards. The mental trauma of experiencing this smell would later combine with a deeply abstract insecurity about the bovine sonority of her married name "Helfenstein." Please do me the honor of welcoming to the stage tonight's expert on all things olfactory, Mrs. Helfenstein.

> (MRS. HELFENSTEIN jumps up and moves quickly to the center front of the stage. She clutches a book to her chest and sways back and forth as she speaks.)

MRS. HELFENSTEIN

We all realize how vividly a long forgotten scene or emotion can be recalled by a bit of orris root, a whiff of sandal wood or a few crumbling rose leaves from an old pot-pourri jar. To many of us the sharp, invigorating smell of box bushes in the sunshine or a lilac hedge in full bloom is a sort of magic which takes us back to the time when we played "hide and seek" in the boxes, and the lilacs bloomed far above our heads.

I think St. John must have had daffodils in mind when on the Isle of Patmos he wrote of "Golden phials, full of odors." There never was a saint or a poet who did not feel his heart up-lifted in a garden.

I believe that after all, the wild things are the sweetest. We have one of the elusive arbutus on the Cathedral grounds and when it blooms in May or early June, I am just like "Ferdinand" – I don't want to do one thing but "sit and smell, and smell the flowers".

We can never be thankful enough for flowers and their fragrance. There is scarcely an occasion in our lives when they have not a message for us. They can cheer and delight, or console and comfort us. Like the rainbow, they are God's special messengers of hope, and when we thank Him for our other blessings, let us not forget His extra gift of "Fragrance in Gardens".

> (MRS. HELFENSTEIN scurries off-stage as SPEAKER takes her place. He addresses the audience again.)

SPEAKER

I can see now that I have marred the evening with my insensate ramblings, please allow me to forgo my long-winded introduction until the end of tonight's last presentation, entitled: "The Green Garden" by our own Mrs. Harvey Beck.

> (MRS. BECK gets up slowly and with purpose. SPEAKER lightly touches her back as she approaches. SPEAKER steps aside.)

MRS. BECK

Let us all have gardens. Ones in which the sense of calm and peace shall in no way be broken. Let us have cool shaded places where we may sit and see the flowers, the birds and bees, and the blue-sky overhead. Let the garden be just near enough to the house to be part of the life of its occupants, where they may go without effort in the day or the evening. Do we know the garden in the evening's half-light when the outlines are softened? It is unlike that of day. Do we know it by moonlight when all green is gone and distant corners are lost in darkness, while perhaps a white blossom stands out, pale and cool, with the moon's rays upon it – its long shadow cast across the pathway? It is at these moments that our gardens are of unspeakable truth to us and we begrudge no care that has gone to their making.

> (MRS. BECK lingers for a moment before stepping down and exiting. SPEAKER takes his place at the podium and waits a moment before talking.)

SPEAKER

I have the unfortunate task of polluting the air with words after such a delicate and profound statement, so let me be brief and to the point, lest I dilute the potency of Mrs. Beck's wisdom.

The details of Mrs. Beck's life seem hardly worth mentioning, the assembled body of the Guilford Garden Club — as you assemble the body of your own helplessly incoherent lives. Forgive me if it seems as though I overstep the boundaries of custom and courtesy at an event such as this one, but I feel compelled to mention that you yourselves are riddled with failure, as blighted as a colony of gypsy moths inside a stand of chestnuts. Need I enumerate? There was that time when, under the influence of alcohol you blurted out a life-altering bit of criticism towards a close companion to whom you subsequently failed to apologize...that time when you learned of an acquaintance of yours contracting a potentially fatal disease — what was that emotion that dangled undefined at the back of your mind? Was it happiness? A kind of gloating at the misfortune of others? It was. I'm sorry, but I've been to too many of these meetings to tell you otherwise. Mrs. Harvey Beck was smarter than most of the people she knew, but it didn't protect her from the deep depression that would color her short life, resulting from an ambiguously sexual relationship with her father. She will be dead a week after uttering the last words of her speech, and those who knew her will turn to the important work of forgetting—eventually nothing will remain of her--the incongruous size of her breasts, the saliva that drips from the corner of her mouth when she sleeps, or what she does in front of her mirror at night. She is suffering the same fate that all of you will suffer—not only to die before you're ready but then to die out and be utterly forgotten—to leave behind only the seeds you planted in your last hours in a half-lit garden, of what you loved enough to leave in your wake, the evidence, to be unearthed in other landscapes, of what you had buried and then let grow into the light.

>(SPEAKER pauses as if lost in thought and just as quickly snaps back to his charming demeanor.)

Ah! I see now that I am late for another appointment. Well then this adjourns the bi-monthly meeting of the Guilford Garden Club. I would like to thank all of the lovely speakers who contributed to the success of the evening. On your way out please take a moment to walk through the garden as you exit the building. Perhaps you may have some suggestions as to what should be planted there. Thank you, and goodnight.

>(SPEAKER quickly closes his binder, tucks it under his arm, and strides off.)

END.

Crusaders

by Tim Paggi

PREMISE:
Near the end of time on planet Baltimore, a few remaining humans confront the digital world and a company that owns everything.

CHARACTERS:

MAGIC CAT   He is magic.

HUNTER   Wears a bright orange sweatsuit and hoodie. He is seeking answers.

OLLIE   A fellow traveller.

AT RISE

> There is a campfire glowing blue. MAGIC CAT and HUNTER sit around it, staring at it as static-y sounds are heard droning all around. They are in an electronic wasteland. Nearby is a rusty street sign post, indicating that this scene takes place on the corner of Barclay and Lanvale.

(The sound dies down.)

MAGIC CAT

I've enjoyed these last couple nights on the journey together. Last night you were telling me that the sun used to be yellow, and was much smaller but much brighter.

HUNTER

It's true, magic cat. But that was a very long time in the past. And there's no proof of it. Just lousy theory.

MAGIC CAT

And you said that reality used to be purely real?

HUNTER

Yes, that's also what they say. That reality hadn't become dented and distorted yet. False information is rampant now. You know how sometimes your toothbrush bites you?

MAGIC CAT

Yeah.

HUNTER

And how sometimes you're riding a bike but then the next second you're eating pudding.

MAGIC CAT

Yeah.

HUNTER

That's infoglitches. They're random. That didn't used to happen when the earth was young.

> (The fire starts to die down.)

MAGIC CAT

Fire's going down. Better throw on another mix cd.

>(The sounds of some long forgotten music crackle in the distance.)

HUNTER

You want to know another thing about the past? There was more than one company too. There used to be lots of companies. And then I think they were outlawed for a few milennia, during the transhumanist world renaissance. But somewhere along the lines of long forgotten history, one company came back. And it grew with power, growing stronger than any company. It owns most of the real world, and the digital world, and a lot of space too.

MAGIC CAT

I'm getting pretty bored with your stories now.

HUNTER

>(to himself)

Sure was a long time ago. When the Earth was young.

>(Enter OLLIE holding a basket. She sits next to the two. She is wearing a headlamp.)

OLLIE

Hey guys. Look at all this amazing stuff I found!

>(she pulls videotapes and Ipods and crystals out of her basket)

MAGIC CAT

That's great.

>(MAGIC CAT takes and eats a tape)

Mmmm. Mmmm.

    (They all start eating things out of the basket and saying "Mmmm!")

HUNTER

I'm going to sleep now. We will need our rest for tomorrow.

OLLIE

Why?

HUNTER

For the journey. Tomorrow our epic quest continues.

    (OLLIE nudges MAGIC CAT)

OLLIE

Oh yeah, the journey. Of course. The big journey.

MAGIC CAT

That endless journey.

HUNTER

Yes. The journey will still be a journey tomorrow. I have a feeling that tomorrow will be the day the reason for the journey will be known to us.

OLLIE

Better be. We've been on this journey forever. For our whole lives. Without knowing why. Guess it's all just for the sake of the adventure, the thrill of it all.

HUNTER

Thank you two for being part of the journey with me.

    (They all go to sleep.)

(They awake the next morning and there is a giant gate behind them that wasn't there before. It is the GATEWAY TO THE DIGITAL WORLD.)

(MAGIC CAT sees the gate first. He approaches it and sniffs it.)

(He sees that it is a gate and tries to open it, but isn't strong enough to do so.)

(He wakes up OLLIE and shows her. She screams out)

OLLIE

Whoa, that wasn't here yesterday!

MAGIC CAT

What is it?

HUNTER

(rising)

What is what?

OLLIE

Holy shit! This is amazing. It's a gateway to the digital world. Just think of all the things in there. We should go in.

HUNTER

No!

OLLIE

Yes, we have to! I bet you never have to eat in there. I bet there's so many amazing informational videos. And communities. And second lives! We have to go in and explore! If we don't then we're just a bunch of useless jerks.

HUNTER

No, I don't trust this. This gateway has nothing to do with our journey.

OLLIE

It might. You don't know if it does or does not have anything to do with it.

HUNTER

I'm the leader here and I said no!

OLLIE

Yes!

HUNTER

No!

OLLIE

Yes!

HUNTER

What if it's a trap planted by the company? Hell we don't even know if this is real or some sort of reality glitch.

OLLIE

No way.

MAGIC CAT

Okay, okay. Stop fighting. There's only one way to resolve this. I'LL go into the digital world.

(OLLIE pulls out a rope.)

OLLIE

Forget that, magic cat. Here's what we'll do. I'll tie this rope around me and tie it to the signpost.

> (OLLIE proceeds to do so as she continues explaining her plan)

If I tug twice at the rope, then you know something is wrong and pull me back.

> (She hands the rope to MAGIC CAT)

Can you do that?

MAGIC CAT

I can do that.

OLLIE

Hunter, you cool?

HUNTER

Fine. Go in.

> (HUNTER draws his sword)

If any monsters come out of there...

OLLIE

There aren't any monsters in the digital world.

> (OLLIE opens the gate and goes halfway through.)

OLLIE

Oh my God, you guys. This is going to be sick! I'm going in! I'm really going into the digital world! Ahhhhh!

(OLLIE goes in. We see a film of her exploring the digital world projected in the background. After thirty seconds or so she begins to get pulled toward something on the screen that looks more or less like a black hole of information. She starts tugging on the rope and screaming in fear.)

MAGIC CAT

She tugged twice!

HUNTER

Pull her back in!

MAGIC CAT

She's heavy, help me!

(HUNTER tries to help MAGIC CAT, but they can't pull OLLIE back in.)

MAGIC CAT

The rope is breaking!

HUNTER

Use your magic powers!

MAGIC CAT

I don't have any magic powers!

(The rope holding OLLIE splits from the signpost. MAGIC CAT and HUNTER try their best to pull OLLIE back in but they can't and they lose hold of the rope which flies into the gate.)

(Then the gate slams shut.)

HUNTER

Shit, fuck, shit. I knew something bad would happen. This gate is probably just a reality glitch.

MAGIC CAT

Maybe the journey continues in there though! Maybe we should continue the adventure in there. It could be amazing. Better than actual reality.

HUNTER

No, I know for a fact that the journey won't lead us into the digital world.

MAGIC CAT

How do you know that? Who told you? You don't even know what the journey is about. Well, fine, unless you can tell me, I'm just going to go in.

HUNTER

No. It's true, I don't know what the journey is all about just yet, but I know that I'm going to find out soon.

MAGIC CAT

Listen, the company is just going to buy us up eventually anyway. It's taking over all of Baltimore. There's no real world left to escape to anyway. We may as well go in. Come on, Hunter, come with me. We'll find Ollie and then we can just do whatever we want. We're lucky, really. Look, I'm just going to stick my head in.

HUNTER

Don't! You'll get sucked in.

>   (HUNTER draws his sword and steps in front of the gateway)

I won't let you.

> (MAGIC CAT breathes fire at HUNTER, knocking him over. MAGIC CAT runs through the portal instantly.)

MAGIC CAT

See you later!

> (MAGIC CAT is gone.)

> (HUNTER stands up, brushing fire off of himself.)

HUNTER

Goddamnit. My only two friends are gone to the digital world. Maybe I should go in. No, no. That's a stupid idea. I'm devoted to the journey. Guess I just gotta go about the journey...alone then.

> (HUNTER gathers his things, kind of putzing around. He continues talking to himself)

I mean, what is reality anyway? Is this world more real than the digital one? What is the digital world? Should I continue spending all of my days trying to figure out what the journey is all about? Or does the true journey begin when I let go of the idea of the journey, and just start living my life the way I want to...maybe...just maybe...I'll go into the gateway...just for a second, yeah.

> (HUNTER approaches the gateway and tries to open it, but it won't open.)

HUNTER

What? What is this bullshit?

> (He tries to pry it open with his sword but it won't budge.)

HUNTER

I give up.

(The gateway disappears.)

(HUNTER's cell phone rings (oh yeah, he has a cell phone))

HUNTER
(before answering)

A call? Can't remember the last time I got a call.

(He answers the phone.)

VOICE ON OTHER END

Hello! This is a friendly representative from the company! Are you an adventurer looking to find the meaning to the journey? but you just can't? Have all of your friends disappeared into the digital world and you're left grasping for straws?

HUNTER

Well, yeah.

VOICE

Have you ever considered working for the company? The company has lots of great options for...

HUNTER
(hanging up)

One thing I definitely know about myself, is I'm not looking to get a job.

THE END

Birdshit

a play in ten minutes or less

by Justin Durel

CHARACTERS

STORK 2	A stork in his early 30's
STORK 3	A stork in his late 30's
MAN	A human male in his late 50's
COW 1	A middle-aged cow
COW 2	A middle-aged cow
ORDER STORKA	stork in his 60's

VARIOUS STORKS IN A CROWD

SCENES

SCENE 1	A stork bar
SCENE 2	A one-room shack
SCENE 3	A field
SCENE 4	The stork parliament

NOTES

NOTE 1: Much of the humor of the piece will rely on the characters' movements, in relation to their species and in contrast to each other. Therefore, the birds will adopt the agitated, twitchy energy and rhythm of birds; the cows will appear heavy and lackadaisical; and the human will have the energy and rhythm of one who sits at a computer for most of his day.

NOTE 2: All genders may be switched.

SCENE 1

> (A bar. STORK 2 converses with STORK 3 over drinks.)

STORK 2

Oh man it was weird, John, weird, I'm tellin' you. It was like talking to an alien, or a sea gull or something, there was just no getting' through, I mean, he's been some place dark, John, and I don't just mean the muck.

STORK 3

Well, sure, can you imagine?

STORK 2

No, I can't! I thought maybe I could, but jeez, after seeing this guy, I don't know, I don't know, it's a whole different bag, John, ya know? I mean, I'm angry, I'm angry as the next stork, but God! after seeing this guy, John, I mean, how can we? How can we keep on doing a thing for these people?!

STORK 3

Well, look, he might have been all messed up, but he's still alive.

STORK 2

Yeah, but he'd rather be dead.

STORK 3

Ah, you don't know that.

STORK 2

You don't know, John, you weren't there, you didn't see. He knows he's supposed to want to be alive and be happy and all that. But he's not, John. I saw it. I saw it in his eyes. Jeez. It was scary.

STORK 3

Well, you know, it's just a part of what happens.

STORK 2

Well what the fuck kind of attitude is that?! This isn't something that just happens.

STORK 3

All right, but it did happen. And what are we gonna do? Just stop delivering babies forever? I mean, c'mon.

>   (STORK 2 stares into his drink, lost. A pause.)

I mean, c'mon, Smit. They just messed up. You've messed up before.

STORK 2

Yeah, but not like this.... You didn't see this bird, John. If you'd a-seen this bird....

>   (A pause. STORK 3 watches STORK 2, then shrugs his shoulders and swigs his drink as the lights fade out.)

SCENE 2

>   (A one-room cabin, perhaps more like a garage, or no, better yet, a shed, a radio shed, but no radio, just the internet. A one room cabin. A keyboard, mouse, and monitor

rest on a desk in the corner. Also, a computer's microphone rests on the desk, and there are papers strewn about too. As the lights come up, a late middle-aged man shuffles over to the desk, his back to the audience. He pulls up his pants, mumbles to himself. He rearranges some papers. He sits down at the desk, moves his computer's mouse and clicks.)

MAN

Uh, hello, guys, welcome to the podcast for, uh...

(He looks at his watch.)

... June 16th. This is a uh, I'll post the link on my website, there's a story here about a blue stork. A blue stork has been born in Biegen, Germany. And this is interesting, not only because it's an, uh, well, an oddity of nature, you know, but also because it hearkens back to an ancient prophecy. Ok? So, uh, to learn about this, we have to go back to the ancient Greeks and, uh, talk about Pegasus. Now Pegasus, as you all know, was a winged horse that, uh, that was the offspring of Posieden, who is god of the sea—take note, the sea—and Medusa, who, as you know, was a gorgon, a monster, with snakes in her hair. If you looked at her you turned to stone, or rather, were petrified, OK? So, uh, as mentioned in the last podcast, we're now in a time where Jupiter will conjunct with Urunas at the star Scha-et, which is in the constellation Pegasus. Uh. And a prophecy comes down to us from the Greeks that states that 'in the the times of overturning'—the end-times—ok?—the beginning of a new era—'in the times of overturning, a blue soul bird will appear,' and uh, that 'soul' bird will be the signal for Pegasus, the winged horse, to alight on earth and stamp his winged hoof, causing 'springs of knowledge' to 'burst forth.' Ok, so now, there's a lot in what I just said there. So, uh, first things first: the blue soul bird. How do we know that blue soul bird is... this stork... this blue stork that has appeared in Bygone Germany? Oh, and by the way I'm saying 'soul' as in s, o, u, l, not s, o, l, e—not sole like alone but soul like, you know, one's soul. Your soul or my soul. Though, this bird is the only bird like this in the world that we have ever heard of, OK?, he is the only bird, the sole stork, that is blue like this. That's very important, and a very important connection to make between that soul/sole interplay. But what's important now, what I'm saying now is that he's a soul—s, o, u, l—bird. Now what does that mean? Well to answer that question we have to do a little research into birds and, uh, their significance to mankind. So, the stork. Well, we all know that storks carry babies to, uh, young married couples, and, uh, sometimes to other people as well. Now, where does this tradition come from? Um... well, I'll tell you, it comes from Ancient Egypt. In Ancient Egypt, the stork was called ba—and you can find all of this on wikipedia in their, uh, Mythology of Storks section. Now ba was not only the ancient Egyptian name for the stork, but it was also the name for, uh... hold on I want to read it to you directly here...

(He shuffles through his papers, finds it.)

'the unique individual character of each human being.'... i.e., his soul. So, the stork is connected with your soul, and, in fact, bears your soul to this earth when you are born. And it's interesting to note that the ancient Egyptian hieroglyph for soul, for the word ba... is a stork with a human's head. And furthermore, its significant to note that the hebrew word for stork, hassida, the devoted one, is where we get the word hassidic.

>(Pause.)

So, here we have these devoted child bearers. Now what child is this blue soul bird bearing? What, uh, what kind of harbinger is this?

>(Pause.)

So, this blue stork appeared in Bygone Germany—by the way that's where the bird appeared, you can look that up too—... and this bird is a harbinger, a signal for Pegasus to return to earth from the stars and stamp his hooves... on the surface of the Earth, which will then cause a spring of knowledge to open up and burst forth. Now this blue stork appeared exactly three days before the Deepwater Horizon rig burst forth into the Gulf of Mexico.

>(Pause.)

Now, uh, I know a lot of you think—Bahh!

>(A stork crashes through the door, splintered wood flying, and slides across the floor, slamming into the opposite wall. A pause. The man is horrified, frozen silent. He begins to babel into the microphone.)

Li-li-li-listeners, I cannot not not begin to tre—

>(The bird begins to stir.)

Ahhhh!

>(The bird gets up, shakes himself off. He checks the contents of his sling and bird-walks over to the once again frozen silent man. The bird offers the man the baby in its sling. The man looks at the baby, looks at the bird, looks at the baby, looks at the bird. The man asks the bird:)

What does this mean?

> (The bird remains motionless. Its only movement is its breathing. Its head is bowed. Slowly, the man takes the child. The bird straightens up clips his bill as if to say "You're welcome," and runs out the door, taking off into the night. The man watches him go, but then the baby cries. He turns toward the baby. The baby cries louder.)

Oh sh—, shh, shh! Oh.

> (He turns this way, then that. What should he do?)

Oh God. Shh... shh....

> (He begins rocking the baby back and forth as it cries. He stares deeply into its face.)

Holy cow...

> (Fade out.)

SCENE 3

> Two cows in a field, casually munching grass, chatting. One of the cows farts.

COW 1

Oop.

COW 2

Aha. Ahahaha.

COW 1

Yep.

COW 2

No, it's good. It's good for you.

COW 1

Yep.

(COW 2 laughs a little more. COW 1 smiles. They continue to eat grass.)

COW 2

So you heard about this blue bird?

COW 1

Huh? No.

COW 2

This blue stork appeared out of nowhere somewhere across the ocean.

COW 1

Oh my.

COW 2

I know.

COW 1

A blue stork.

COW 2

Yeah.

COW 1

A little odd.

                        COW 2

I know.

(A pause.)

                        COW 1

Well what's the deal with it?

                        COW 2

I don't know, it's just a blue stork.

                        COW 1

Huh. Well I suppose it's not that odd. My great aunt once gave birth to a calf that had no spots.

                        COW 2

Oh, well, sure. That happens sometimes. But a blue stork!

                        COW 1

Well, I don't know, you know, it's all just abnormalities in nature.

                        COW 2

A mistake.

                        COW 1

Yeah.

(A pause.)

Or I don't know, maybe it's on purpose. Who knows, really?

(COW 2 nods in agreement.)

                        COW 2

Well anyway, it's rather interesting.

COW 1

Well sure.

(A pause.)

Any relation to the, uh, the big mess?

COW 2

Oh who knows.

COW 1

(Nodding agreement.)

Ah.

(COW 2 farts.)

COW 2

Ahp!

COW 1

Aha, ahahaha.

COW 2

Ahahahaha.

COW 1

It's your turn now,

COW 2

Yeah, ahaha, yeah....

(A pause. Fade out.)

SCENE 4

> A rabble of clipping bills, quiet awkward squawks, and shouting. Lights up on a group of official storks. The one in the middle has a gavel, which he is pounding.

ORDER STORK

Order! Order! We need order! Now we can't proceed unless we have order! Now the dock has heard your concerns regarding the severity of this disgraceful situation. And I believe we have made it perfectly clear that we all agree that this kind of thing must never happen again. But we will not be able to move forward if we do not refrain from bringing up the sludge!

> (Shouts, clips, squawks.)

Now, now, we all know what the sludge has done. We all know the horror. We even now know of the undeniable traumatic experiences of the survivors, and we are beginning to see how this has irrevocably affected the stream of their lives. But what we do not know is: Who is to blame.

> (Shouts, clips, squawks.)

Now, now there is disagreement on this! Let me finish, let me finish!

> (The crowd quiets down. He pauses.)

We are yet to decide whom we blame... and how we will deal with them. Now, some of you want to stop delivering babies all together.

> (Clips, cheers.)

I strongly caution against this. We have born these precious, unique souls for as long as any stork can remember. And now is not the time to start making drastic decisions! In times of volatility, we must remain cautious and reasonable. We cannot allow this mistake—

> (Clips, boos, storks yelling "Mistake?!")

Look, however you slice it, this thing—in the entire history of our species—this thing is a relatively small blip, and it is not a reason...

> (Clips, shouts. ORDER PELICAN shouts over the shouts.)

... it is not a valid reason to break the covenant. Now listen!

> (The crowd quiets down again.)

This covenant has worked for for as long as anyone can remember, and it has seen and experienced much worse than this fiasco. And there is nothing about this situation that suggests that things need to change on such a drastic level as to stop delivering babies entirely!

A VOICE IN THE CROWD

What about the blue bird?

VARIOUS VOICES IN THE CROWD

Yes what about the blue bird? Yeah, the blue bird!

ORDER STORK

All right, all right, this blue stork! As you all know, a blue stork appeared in flight over the continent some months ago. Since then she has taken up residence in Germany, has built a nest, and is living a peaceful life there, doing her duty by day, and living her life by night. Now, regarding her pigmentation.... It is the opinion of the order that her color is the cause of an anomalous genetic mutation, much like the two-headed tern recently born in Labrador, and nothing more!

> (Shouts, clips, a ruckus.)

A VOICE IN THE CROWD

Enough of this nonsense! No more babies!

> (Cheers, excited clipping of bills. The crowd begins to chant "No more babies! No more babies!)

THE CROWD

No more babies! No more babies!

ORDER STORK

Now order! Order!

> (The storks engulf the official storks, chanting, going mad, as ORDER STORK yells for order. ORDER STORK stretches his wings up, trying to escape, but he is held down by the enveloping mob. Fade out.)

END OF PLAY

Getting Nailed Down

by Dina Kelberman

CAST (in order of apperance)

Blue Balloon	a person dressed as a long, narrow, blue balloon
Hermaine	wears yellow
Explode	wears grey
Hermaine II	another version of Hermaine (looks identical)
Armand	wears red
Hermaine Dummy	an actual dummy
Hermaine Dummy II (looks identical)	a living version of the Hermaine Dummy
Swindly	a dolphin

(Yoga positions are in bold)

SCENE I

(Scene opens w/ spotlight fade up on BLUE BALLOON at far stage right, jiggling arms and legs and making contented faces. Spotlight widens to show HERMAINE laying down nearby, flat on back, arms and legs splayed open, staring up. EXPLODE is performing Reiki on HERMAINE.)

EXPLODE

Okay . . . I think this time it's gonna work.

HERMAINE

I —

(is immediately cut off by EXPLODE)

EXPLODE

DON'T SAY ANYTHING!

(begins to resume but it's quickly apparent that it's not working anymore)

Great. It's broken.

(stands up)

It's not my fault. You suck at this. You're just super not-transcendent and it's annoying.

HERMAINE

Is —

(is immediately cut off by EXPLODE)

EXPLODE

Ohmygodwhatthehell? DON'T TALK.

(HERMAINE makes an "I don't know what to do then" face.)

EXPLODE

(frustrated)

Maybe this wasn't a good idea. Maybe we're not ready for this. Maybe it's too soon.

> (HERMAINE makes another face in an attempt to convey emotion without speaking.)

EXPLODE

(tired)

I should just go. I'll just get my stuff and go . . . sorry. I mean, you know, maybe we can do this some other time. Sorry. I just . . .you said you were gonna make an effort.

> (EXPLODE goes over to BLUE BALLOON and gently guides BB off stage left. HERMAINE remains, unmoving. HERMAINE closes eyes.)

> (Spotlight fades up on stage left. HERMAINE II is doing a headstand. Both spotlights fade down.)

SCENE II

> (Spotlight fades up on stage right. HERMAINE lays down, flat on back, arms and legs splayed open, staring up. ARMAND is performing Reiki on HERMAINE.)

ARMAND

Do you feel anything?

HERMAINE

I don't know.

ARMAND

Is it working? Is this working??

HERMAINE

I don't know! You don't know?

ARMAND

Oh my god am I hurting you?? Am I powerful??

HERMAINE

What?

ARMAND

Tell me if you can feel this.

> (Does something specific)

HERMAINE

Oh . . . yeah it . . . wait . . . was it . . . that? Which was it?

> (ARMAND gives some kind of "what, are you kidding me?" look to HERMAINE. HERMAINE is embarrassed.)

HERMAINE

Am I doing a bad job?

ARMAND

Kind of. Yeah.

HERMAINE

I get that a lot.

ARMAND

I just feel like you're not taking me seriously.

HERMAINE

No I am!

ARMAND

Well one of us isn't taking the other one seriously. That's for sure.

(HERMAINE looks askance.)

ARMAND

It's like . . . it's like your mirror neurons aren't taking me seriously.

HERMAINE

I don't think that's possible.

ARMAND

Are you colorblind?

HERMAINE

What's that mean?

ARMAND

Colors.

HERMAINE

What?

ARMAND

COLORS.

HERMAINE

Like what?

ARMAND

Well, you know round?

HERMAINE

Oh yeah! I love round!

ARMAND

You know pointy?

HERMAINE

Yeah.

ARMAND

Well it's like them, but it's another one, a different kind. And it's see-through.

> (HERMAINE nods, thinking about this deeply. Spotlight fades up stage left.)
>
> (HERMAINE II is lying identically to HERMAINE. Over the course of the next couple lines HERMAINE II gets into the **wheel** and holds till the end of the scene.)

ARMAND

(stands up)

Ok, well, I'll bring that form over to your house for you to sign ok? I think if we do like one more session that's all the hours I need.

HERMAINE

(distracted, still concentrating)

Yeah. Okay.

(ARMAND exits stage left. HERMAINE stares straight up, thinking hard.)

HERMAINE

Yellow.

(Both spotlights fade down.)

SCENE III

(Spotlight fades up stage right. ARMAND kneels above a dummy version of HERMAINE, performing Reiki on it. EXPLODE stands above them with a clipboard, observing. ARMAND is wearing some kind of ridiculous head-garb or something.)

ARMAND

... and you will feel your inner fingers respond. Your inner fingers are loosening.

EXPLODE

Very good.

(makes a mark on the clipboard.)

ARMAND

(visibly encouraged)

Waggle your inner fingers. Feel them waggle.

(EXPLODE nods and makes more clipboard marks.)

(ARMAND begins to make gestures above the HERMAINE dummy's legs, as if lifting them invisibly.)

ARMAND

Your fingers. Your feet.

(Spotlight fades up on stage left. HERMAINE DUMMY II is doing a **headstand**. ARMAND looks up at EXPLODE, finished.)

EXPLODE

Very good.

(ARMAND is happy. Both spotlights fade down.)

SCENE IV

(Spotlight fades up stage left. HERMAINE II wears a yellow swim cap and goggles. SWINDLY enters, swimming alongside HERMAINE II. They acknowledge each other with nods and swim for a bit without speaking. They are exercising.)

SWINDLY

(exuberantly friendly)

I'm tired! You tired? This is EXHAUSTING!

HERMAINE II

I don't know. I can't tell.

SWINDLY

God I'm EXHAUSTED! I'm so TIRED! It's like, I wish I was, like – dead!

HERMAINE II

That must be very difficult for you.

SWINDLY

Oh man, not me! I love this feeling!

> (suddenly feeling competitive)

Who can swim faster?

> (SWINDLY starts swimming more ferociously, HERMAINE II struggles to keep up.)

SWINDLY

Ha!

> (taking it down a notch, triumphantly)

I knew it was me.

HERMAINE II

Well this is just recreational for me.

SWINDLY

Yeah, me too, me too. But faster.

> (Spotlight fades up stage right. HERMAINE laying in the same spot on the stage, in the same way, legs and arms out, staring at ceiling. A

beach towel is under HERMAINE'S bod. A beachball is next to HERMAINE'S head. HERMAINE is wearing sunglasses.)

(ARMAND, EXPLODE and BLUE BALLOON enter from stage left. They both are also wearing sunglasses. EXPLODE ushers BLUE BALLOON back into the same spot from before, and BB makes floaty movements again. Throughout the scene, BLUE BALLOON eyes the beachball with great interest. ARMAND and EXPLODE lay out their towels near but not with, HERMAINE.)

EXPLODE

Ohmygod, that tea ceremony was the fucking shit! Amiright?

ARMAND

Yeah! Yeah, I totally thought so!

EXPLODE

Yessssssssssssssss!

    (pumps fist in that way)

They high-five.

(HERMAINE closes eyes tight, tighter. HERMAINE II and SWINDLY swim faster. ARMAND and EXPLODE are having a great time together. They put suntan lotion on each other's backs.)

SWINDLY

    (Still swimming, looks up at the sky)

Hey, should we be wearing suntan lotion?

HERMAINE II

(Still swimming)

I don't think it matters here.

SWINDLY

(Stops swimming. HERMAINE II stops too)

It's important to protect yourself. Don't be a hero.

(At this point BLUE BALLOON is overcome with curiosity and begins handling the beachball.)

HERMAINE II

Well, okay. Here, I guess, I'll put it on –

(HERMAINE II is cut off by the sound of the beachball popping)

(Both spotlights abruptly down.)

SCENE V

(Spotlight fades up on stage right and stage left simultaneously. HERMAINE lies as before, stage right. A blanket is over HERMAINE'S bod. A lamp is next to HERMAINE'S head. HERMAINE II is stage left, sitting cross-legged on the floor in front of a tv, playing Tetris.)

HERMAINE

How are we doing?

HERMAINE II

> (never stops looking at screen and playing Tetris during this conversation)

Good. Too soon to tell though. You know.

HERMAINE

What level are we on now?

HERMAINE II

13. I'm feeling pretty good about things but you know, it's all about level 19.

HERMAINE

I know.

> (Beat)

HERMAINE

Do you think we could play chess again some time?

HERMAINE II

I hated that.

HERMAINE

Yeah but, like, I bet if we just kept trying we could get better at it and then it would suck less. And like . . . chess is for smart people.

HERMAINE II

Tetris is for smart people too.

HERMAINE

Yeah but I never get to play.

HERMAINE II

That's cause you fuck the whole thing up.

HERMAINE

I know.

> (Beat. Suddenly HERMAINE II becomes visibly more stressed out and frantic in the gameplay.)

HERMAINE

Oh no!

> (HERMAINE II comes to frantic conclusion, having lost the game.)

HERMAINE II

Shit!!!

HERMAINE

Ok. It's ok. Just breathe. Start over.

SCENE VI

> (Spotlight fades up stage right. HERMAINE lays as before. Spotlight fades up stage left. HERMAINE II is attempting to perform the **scorpion**, but is having a hard time.)

                    HERMAINE

                              (With quiet concentration. Eyes
                              open)

Blue.

                    (HERMAINE II struggles.)

                              HERMAINE

Blue.

                    (HERMAINE II struggles, becoming increasingly
                    discouraged.)

                              HERMAINE

Blue.

                    (HERMAINE II continues to struggle, and is
                    basically falling over as the spotlight fades down
                    on stage left.)

                              HERMAINE

                                        (Abandoning concentration)

Dicks.

          (Spotlight fades down on stage right.)

SCENE VII

                              (Scene opens w/
                              spotlight fade up on
                              BLUE BALLOON at far
                              stage right, jiggling
                              arms and legs and
                              making contented faces.
                              Spotlight widens to
                              show HERMAINE

laying down nearby, flat on back, arms and legs splayed open, staring up. EXPLODE is performing Reiki on HERMAINE.)

HERMAINE

Thanks for doing this, I really want it to work this time.

EXPLODE

Well, hopefully that's true. I mean, I can only do so much of this myself, you know?

HERMAINE

I know, I know. I'm really in it for the long haul this time, I mean it.

EXPLODE

Well, your aspect seems more open-minded than before . . . but I'm still having a hard time reading your tone quality . . . have you been taking bird pollen supplements?

HERMAINE

Huh?

EXPLODE

(Slightly exhasperated)

Do you even read the newspaper?

HERMAINE

I've been blacking out a lot lately, so I'm not really sure.

EXPLODE

Well you certainly haven't been wearing enough feather or feather-type garb. First impressions count, you know? In fact, I guess now they count twice as much.

HERMAINE

Really?

EXPLODE

YES. That happened like a week ago! Man, you are so out of it.

HERMAINE

Well it's just i've been trying to break this tetris world record and teach myself to see colors so. . . I guess I've been kind of distracted.

> (EXPLODE looks at HERMAINE with disapproval)

So yeah okay, I'll . . . I'll get some feathers.

> (Beat)

HERMAINE

Do . . . do they have to be real feathers?

EXPLODE

> (Freaking out)

WHAT DO YOU THINK THIS IS?? THIS IS REAL!!! SHIT!!! MOTHERFUCKER!!! WHY DO YOU PULL SHIT BULLSHIT EVERY TIME I TRY TO HELP YOU GET OUT OF THE FUCKING BOX??? WHY CAN'T YOU JUST PULL ONE IOTA OF FUCKING COSMIC EFFORT OUT OF YOUR FUCKING ASS FOR FIVE SEC –

(BLUE BALLOON pops. EXPLODE is visibly horrified and physically distraught.)

EXPLODE

MY SPIRIT ANIMAL!!!! FUCKING SHIT!!!!!!

HERMAINE

Oh my god! Are you –

(Spotlight quickly down.)

SCENE VIII

(Spotlight fades up on stage right and stage left simultaneously. HERMAINE lies as before, stage right. HERMAINE is covered in paper feathers. A lamp is next to HERMAINE'S head. HERMAINE II is stage left, sitting cross-legged on the floor in front of a TV, playing Tetris.)

(HERMAINE II plays the game for a bit, then looks over at HERMAINE.)

HERMAINE II

You know, I think it's actually helping.

(HERMAINE smiles.)

THE END

An Annotated Guide to a Normal Conversation, or: This Cake Is Delicious!

by Cricket Arrison

Characters

Bess   A normal woman. Friends with Lana.

Lana   A normal woman. Friends with Bess.

Worm   A worm.

Teapot   A teapot.

Pi   Pie.

The scene titles should be somehow conveyed to the audience, via. projection, someone walking across the state with signs, or saying them out loud, or some other exciting way heretofore unknown to theater-going audiences

Scene One: A Normal Conversation

> (A lovely kitchen. Bess is fetching pieces of cake for Lana.)

BESS

Cake?

LANA

Oh my gosh, that's beautiful!

> (A small sob is heard from under the table. Neither Bess nor Lana hears it at all, or reacts in any way.)

BESS

Oh, thanks! I've been really getting into baking lately!

(Flicks at icing on cake)

LANA

Cool. I can't bake at all. I don't know how you do it!

BESS

Well, I've had a lot of practice.

LANA

Yeah?

BESS

Yeah, I guess.

(Pause. Bite of cake.)

LANA

Mmm, it's really good.

BESS

Thanks!

(Pause)

LANA

So, how's your job?

BESS

Oh, it's good. You know. Stressful, but I like it, so that's good.

LANA

That's great!

BESS

Yeah, I'm really happy.

LANA

Cool.

BESS

What about yours? Is your boss still completely evil?

LANA

OH MY GOD. I DON'T EVEN WANT TO TALK ABOUT IT. IT'S TAKING OVER MY BRAIN. IT'S JUST – WHERE DO PEOPLE LIKE THAT COME FROM, YOU KNOW? SHE'S SO MANIPULATIVE! IT COULD BE SUCH AN AMAZING PLACE TO WORK, BUT SHE TREATS HER EMPLOYEES LIKE GARBAGE...

BESS

Yeah, I know.

LANA

But enough about that. It makes me so mad, how all I talk about is work. But how can I not? The other day she decided that we have to take down all of the shirts at the end of the day, refold them, and put them back on the shelves.

BESS

No way.

LANA

Yes! Isn't that insane?

BESS

She's really terrible.

LANA

I mean, WHO is really going to care that all of the shirts are folded exactly the same. Even if they don't get touched at all during the shift, we have to take them down, and refold them, and put them back up. It's such an exercise in futility. But I really don't want to talk about work.

BESS

Yeah.

LANA

It's just that I hate how miserable it makes me, which just makes me more miserable. It's a vicious cycle. But if I quit, my next job will just make me even more miserable.

BESS

You don't know that.

LANA

Yes, I do. That's her power over everyone.

(Pause. Teapot crashes to the floor)

BESS

That was weird.

LANA

How did that happen?

(Pause)

LANA

This cake is delicious!

BESS

Yes.

(Brushes crumbs off herself.)

Scene Two: Did You Leave the Oven On When You Left the House?

> A lovely kitchen. Bess is fetching pieces of cake for Lana. The physicality of this scene should replicate the actions of Scene One as precisely as possible. The same tone of sweet politeness should also be maintained, with smiles throughout, even when the words are distressed. Unless otherwise indicated, Bess and Lana don't hear or react to what the other person is saying in this scene.

BESS

(Offering cake to Lana)

Eeeeeeeeew!

LANA

> (Takes cake, smiling politely.)

Fuck. Oh fuck. FuckFuckFuck.

> (A small sob is heard from under the table. Neither Bess nor Lana hears it at all, or reacts in any way.)

BESS

God is that a bug in the frosting? I hope she doesn't see it.

> (Flicks at icing to get rid of bug.)

LANA

Fuck I didn't call for Gram's birthday oh my GOD i'm such a fuckup.

BESS

Did she notice the weird thing on my chin?

LANA

Fuck.

BESS

Oh god it itches.

> (Pause. Bite of cake.)

LANA: Should I call her now? Probably not. Shit. I am the worst person.

BESS

I want to put my face in the cake!!! What a strange impulse. But I do. But I won't.

LANA

Sickly sweet muck.

BESS

If I put my face in the cake she couldn't see my weird chin thing.

(Pause)

LANA

So I've been thinking about antelope! Oh god what kind of a terrible conversation starter is that? But it's true, I have! Shit.

(To Bess)

So how's your job?

(To herself again.)

LAME thing to say. Lame!

BESS

I don't know how I feel about anything, but I'll say "It's good," because that typically pleases people.

("It's good" is delivered to Lana as if it were part of a normal conversation – the rest is to herself.)

LANA

I shouldn't be here.

BESS

(To Lana)

Yeah, I'm really happy.

(To herself)

Am I really happy?

LANA

Fuck.

BESS

What a strange day today is. I feel like there's something I should be noticing but I can't tell what it is.

LANA

RRRAWWWR! I HATE MY JOB.

BESS

Oh man, I got her talking about her job again. Time to see how hard I can bite my tongue without yelling!

LANA

(Getting increasingly excited to be talking about this.)

My job my job my job my job my job my job my job my job my job my job my job .

(BESS is biting her tongue harder and harder, starting to make muffled noises of pain.)

LANA

Jobby job job job job jobster. Job! Jobby JOBB JOB JOB JOB Worky work. Job Job.

BESS

(Finally can't take it and screams in pain)

AAAAAAAAA! Whew. That felt good.

LANA

MY JOB!!

>(Pause. Teapot crashes to the floor. Bess and Lana notice each other for the first time in a while.)

BESS

That was weird.

LANA

How did that happen?

>(Pause)

LANA

This cake sucks.

BESS

I love this cake.

>(Brushes crumbs off herself.)

Scene Three: Bet You Didn't Know You Had It In You

LANA

>(Seated at the table, quietly, to herself, while carefully inspecting her foot, which she is cradling in her hands.)

What a pretty foot! Pretty toes, pretty pretty foot. What a pretty foot. What's afoot in the world today? Foot, you really nailed it! You're so on the ball! What an amazing feat you accomplished!

You're the sole thing in this world that understands me. And stands under me!

> (Laughs)
>
> (BESS hops around the room like a monkey, making monkey noises.)
>
> (LANA falls off her chair, laughs maniacally. Rolls around on the floor with her foot in hand.)
>
> (A small sob is heard from under the table. Neither Bess nor Lana hears it at all, or reacts in any way.)

BESS

> (Hops up to Lana)

YOU ARE MY PRISONER IN THE KINGDOM. I AM QUEEN, YOU ARE A KNOW-NOTHING LAZY SONOFABITCH. SOME DAY THE WORLD WILL KNOW THIS AS I KNOW IT NOW, AS TRUTH.

LANA

My butt is itchy.

BESS

I didn't mean it! You're the only one who understands me!

> (Bess kisses Lana, passionately. Lana slaps Bess.)

LANA

How unexpected! Here I thought I was here merely to sample baked goods. Or baked bads, in this instance. Oh well!

> (Lana kisses Bess and Bess slaps Lana.)

BESS

Lately I have dreamed so often of ladybugs and their hard wings. I don't know why I have the desire to put them in my mouth and crunch them. Am I normal?

LANA

The Antelope, my friend, is a fairer creature than any bug, be it lady or not. I don't wish to listen to your self-conscious assessments of your insect chomping fantasies. Eat a fucking lady bug, or don't!

(Teapot crashes to the floor)

BESS

Well, that was embarrassing. I want some goddamed cake.

(Eats some cake, then brushes crumbs from herself.)

Scene Four: What You Probably Didn't Notice (abridged)

(A worm crawls out, along the front of the stage, and slowly worms its way across. Along the way it pauses to eat a crumb that Bess brushes off herself, in slow motion. Bess and Lana act out the end of the original scene, in slow motion. This should take 30 seconds, maybe, during which all they get out is:)

LANA

Thhhhhhhhhhiiiiiiiiiisssssssssss
caaaaaaaaaaaaaaaaaaaaaaaaaaaaaake
iiiiiiiiiiiiiiiissssssssssssssssss ddddddeeeeeeliiiiiciiouuuuusss

BESS

Yyyyyyyyyyyyyeeeeeeeeeeeeeeeeeeeeeeesssssssssssssssssssssssss ssssssssss.

Scene Five: Interlude

> (Bess is sobbing,
> holding the cake, curled
> up in Lana's lap.)

BESS

It's just... It's just.... It's just cake! You know? I just wanted to make you some cake! But... I feel so helpless. Cake? Cake!?! The world's in flames and my answer is... Cake?! I want to do something with my life, I want to be somebody, but I just... I just.... All I have is this cake!

LANA

Ssh, shh, it's OK. It's good cake. I love this cake.

BESS

You love the cake?

LANA

Yes. I love the cake. It's delicious. It means the world to me that you baked me this cake. The most important thing is this cake.

BESS

> (Beginning to feel better.)

I'm glad you like it.

                    LANA

                (Really means it.)

This cake... is DELICIOUS!

Scene Six: Tempest in a Teapot

> (BESS and LANA act out a slightly shortened version of the physical actions of the first scene. Meanwhile, an actor dressed as a giant teapot creeps on stage. The actor's face should be visible in the costume, and there is a gag in her mouth. She does not look happy. She grows progressively more and more panicked throughout the conversation, clumsily hopping around the scene trying to get the gag out until eventually it gets to the point of the scene where there is the sound of crashing china. At that point, the teapot spits out the gag, and topples over, in some form of teapot suicide. Her eyes

close. A blissful smile spreads across her face.)

LANA

This cake is delicious.

BESS

Yes.

Scene Seven: Put It All Together, and What Do You Get?

BESS

(Offering cake to Lana)

Cake? Cake? EEEEEW

LANA

Oh, you! FUCK that's my beautiful foot, on the ball!

(A small sob is heard from under the table. Neither Bess nor Lana hears it at all, or reacts in any way.)

BESS

Oh, thanks! God I've – excuse me - been getting into bug lately!

(makes monkey noise)

LANA

Cool. I can't bake at all. Gran – FUCK!

(maniacal laugh)

I don't know how you do it! A time like this!

BESS

Yeah, I itches. Understand me! Cake.

(Pause. Bite of cake.)

LANA

So, what's wrong with your sickly muck, antelope conversation starter?

BESS

Oh, Stressful, I feel anything at all.

LANA

Shouldn't I be Great? It's all the same.

BESS

I bit my yelling tongue. Mmmm beautiful lamp bugs.

LANA

Yes! Jobby! Isn't that job?

BESS

She's really — AAAAAAAAAAAAAAA!

LANA

I mean, WHO is fooling every glance in the mirror? Equality: all of the shirts are folded exactly the same. You could have used that exercise in futility.

BESS

Yeah. Ladybug crunch. Honest.

LANA

It's just that I hate how miserable self-conscious antelope assessments make me. Honest.

BESS

You don't deceive hypocrites.

LANA

Yes, I do. That's her power over never, ever everyone world.

(Teapot enters, crashes to the floor)

BESS

Prisoners are preferable.

LANA

But how did that happen?

(pause)

LANA

This cake is Deeeeeeeeeeliiiiiiiiiiicccccccccioooooooooooooooouuuuuuuuuuuuuuuuuusssssssssssss.

(Worm crawls across)

BESS

Yes. Goddamned cake. Brushes crumbs off herself.

Scene Eight: But This Is What's Really Behind it All

(A lovely kitchen. Bess is fetching pieces of cake for Lana)

BESS

Cake?

LANA

Oh my gosh, that's beautiful!

> (Pi cries, quietly. Bess and Lana hear the sobs and lift the table cloth. Pi is sitting under there, looking confused to have been found out.)

BESS

Oh!

LANA

Where did you come from?

BESS

Who are you?

PI

I'm Pi. But I'm nobody. You don't need to pay attention to me.

LANA

Don't be humble, Pi. Tell us about yourself.

PI

> (Urgently, a bit afraid.)

Well, you're not supposed to be able to see me. I don't know how that happened. But you should know by now that every force in the universe must be balanced. So, every time a cake is made, a Pi is also born, to keep things balanced. It's a terrible life. To sit idly by while you devour that foul stuff

> (points at the cake)

never being able to say anything about it.

BESS

Oh my god, I had no idea!

LANA

What can we do to make it right?

PI

Eat me instead.

BESS

Eat you?

PI

Yes. I'm delicious.

LANA

But... It seems so wrong, somehow.

>（PI Starts to cry again.）

BESS

Well, I guess if you really want us to...

LANA

Well... If you do really want us to, after all that cake we ate... Really, I think it's the least we can do.

PI

REALLY?!?!

>(Pi lays down on the table and looks up at them expectantly, sobs turning to a giant smile. Bess and Lana pick up knives and forks begin to eat

Pi, who giggles, while Bess and Lana make noisy chewing sounds, smack their lips, and mutter admiring comments about how delicious Pi is as the lights fade, such as:)

BESS

Mmmmmmmm, delicious - you really take the cake, Pi – eer, I mean...

LANA

Stop trying to butter him up. This is no trifling matter.

BESS

I'm not, I just think he's delicious. I love how tart he is.

LANA

He's not a tart, he's a pie!

BESS

So sue me!

LANA

It's about time we got some tort reform around here.

BESS

The rest of the world doesn't know what they're missing. Let them eat cake!!! It's pie for me.

The Mysterious Occurrence in the House of Camille; 2010 World Almanac

By Ric Royer

Some notable floods:

1703, Awa Japan.

1889, Johnstown, PA

1903, June 15, Heppner, OR I'm sorry, it will impossible - in only ten minutes a million years for us to discover and understand the strange event that took place in the House of Camille in 1940 1612, 2067. But what we can do in our allotted time is discuss the various details surrounding the event, like the color of the velvet curtains red, blue, the outline of a human hand, traced onto paper, by a child, the breeze, the family photographs that hung on the wall and the characters involved in the scene: acorns, disaster, crystal chandelier. Family secrets. As you can see here, there were a number of suspicious people involved in the mysterious occurrence in the house of Camille. These are not the actual people, but representations of them. We saw something we shouldn't have What. is in. your mouth? They open there mouths wide. I have the urge to utter: "And here we go". But I must restrain myself. If I begin to discuss the mysterious events I could go on and on until the end of me. But I must only circumnavigate, beat around the bush, talk in circles and express myself indirectly. There was a death. That much is certain. And nobody dies of natural causes unless there is murder involved. Oh, and did I mention that there had also been some sex with animals? Some notable earthquakes: 1892, Galveston, Texas, 1902, San Diego, California, 1990, Bombay, India, It was near dawn, midnight, never. There was a haze that softened the horizon and two young women, a dog, 10 dogs, a lizard. A porn horse, the creaking of an old wooden home; the women were feeling nostalgic, adventurous, etcetera. I'm feeling nostalgic, murderous, etc. Everything was calm. Fin de siècle typography. Mornings like this have a flair for the dramatic. I can barely contain myself. I am Satan, Jesus Christ, Jesus Christ... "Jesus Christ, Jesus Christ", was the cry heard throughout the neighborhood. Crayon drawings on the fridge. This is a big house, a silent house, a haunted house where anything can happen and when it does it can stay there forever. I have the urge to shout "And here we go", but if I do I should be chased, not in jest, but to be silenced, like when they say "an angry mob silenced that man". For I have eaten the forbidden noodles, white grapes. The scene at the House of Camille is unrepeatable, not because of its excess, but because the event was layered, like my memory of the pig men, or the day the universe ended. A life was lost that night, a love was born and three different species of animals were violated. Keep your hands to yourself! The clock struck midnight and... Phases of the moon: Gibbous, Full, other. Whatever happened, it sure was evil. Ladies all three lean their faces close to each other, do you find me attractive? Maybe kewpie dolls. Seriously, was I born well? Would you kiss me if you could? Kissing sound. A belch. Image of horrible house is projected. I drew this house, isn't it swell? This is not the actual house of Camille, but a representation of it. Does it turn you on, representation? The contours, the detail, the distance and lack of content? Do aesthetics arouse you? Are you turned on when you turn your attention to the way a thing looks, the way it's shaped, the impeccably graceful way that it implies movement? Ooh- Let's play a game. No, not now. Let's play a game. We can't not with the little girl in the other room, it's not right. Let's play a game. And then they played a game, and a terrible thing happened. Some people might say that the thing that happened wasn't terrible, but just "the way things go", and others yet may say that children deserve it, others may say still that these kinds of things, like the kind of thing that happened in the house of Camille, the woods 1940, nightly, are the kinds of things that need to happen every so often in order to relieve the darkness of the collective consciousness. It is natural, such things are natural. But most people would say it was hideous, heinous, awful and repugnant. A terrible thing happened, they would say. Although some of the parties involved thought that the mysterious events were rather sacred, salvific and neat. The clock struck midnight and... Two women entered the house of Camille on April 15th 1974, it was Guy Fawkes Day, one woman was told it was haunted, the other woman was told it was haunted by the other woman. Was someone stabbed? They broke in on a dare they heard noises they saw shadowy figures in the distance they tasted salt in their mouths, they had flashbacks to memories that were not theirs they tried to leave they found a small egg in each of their mouths that held inside of it a stone a living stone can you believe it a living stone one was red one was black. Did someone get stabbed? They looked in each room and in each they felt an obsessive nostalgia, top ten countries in overall child well-being 1. Netherlands 2. Sweden 3. Denmark, they wondered if this had actually been the house of their birth and if not, if it could be. Was it a cop? The feeling of nostalgia grew stronger and stronger, until it became unbound passion and they adopted the house as their universe, the house took them as their slaves, a child must be sacrificed, a lamb prodded, lesbian imagery, im losing it, im losing it, Did a cop get stabbed?, it is hazy now, wait its coming back to me, this is not what happened in the house of Camille but what else happened. or a kid? People were hurt, and animals destroyed, that hearts and minds torn asunder, and clothing soiled, and mud puppies lost. Something had to have happened first for this to have happened second. Demons, bestiality, honk-honk. Children got messed up, Vegas, Aeroplanes, bombs, drugs, classical music and shards of glass poked, poke, poking. Ahh, a little brandy. the ghosts of two young girls. Matricide, fratricide, suicide, patricide, infanticide, megacide. Hmm.

I'm afraid to go to go in my own house

in my own house, in my own house

I'm afraid to go to go in my own house

It houses too many secrets.

I'm sorry, it would be impossible for me to tell you about the mysterious event that occurred in the house of Camille. There are no words to describe something so strange and so stylish. It's too, too, too. Memorable moments in human space flight: Number one.

www.ingramcontent.com/pod-product-compliance
Lightning Source LLC
Chambersburg PA
CBHW071308060426
42444CB00034B/1647